Further Praise for *B*

"A warm and inviting reflection on the art and craft of teaching, written by a master educator, this book offers both beginning teachers and veterans insights into how to inspire students to go beyond test scores and numbers. An important work in these troubled educational times."

—**Kate Krahl**, history department, Scarsdale High School

"*Bringing History Home* is a godsend for educators looking for ways to inspire their students and foster a love of learning about the past. Bill Schechter beautifully chronicles how he and his students brought history to life by becoming musicologists, theater directors, Thoreau cabin builders, mural painters, mock trial judges, tour guides, poets, sociologists, and agents of change. Ultimately, Schechter's creative ideas, humorous stories, and life lessons highlight why we need our schools to be innovative, supportive academic communities instead of test prep factories."

—**Dan Peppercon**, author of *Creative Adventures in Social Studies*, and history teacher/curriculum coordinator, E. W. Thurston Junior High School

"Schechter is clearly the kind of teacher that we were lucky to have once or twice in our school career and that we fervently hope our children (and grandchildren) will encounter. Bill Schechter's inspiring and engrossing book reminds us that a transformative public education is not about textbooks, curricula, and tests. It's about humans, teachers, and students connecting and sharing challenging ideas and stories. It's a clarion call to give today's teachers the resources and autonomy to make their classrooms come alive."

—**Lisa Guisbond**, director, Citizens for Public Schools, Boston, MA

"Bill Schechter is the master teacher of bringing history home. I regard public schools as the citadels of America's Democracy, and the social studies classroom as the crucible in which the narrative of our nation's civic creed it conjured up, allowing students to gain a deep understanding, and in the words of Dr. King, 'to one day live out the true meaning of its creed.' This book is a 'must-read' for any high school history teacher determined to enliven social studies and inspire their students' imagination to what is truly possible in living out the American Dream."

—**Larry Aaronson**, history department,
Cambridge Rindge and Latin High School

"In Schechter's classroom, teachers are set free to design lessons that engage young people and encourage critical thinking. Students are awakened to the urgency of historical debate. So engaged, they may remember a single lesson for their entire lives. Is this for real? Very much so. I know because I was his student."

—**Robin Espinola**, Emmy-nominated producer of historical films for PBS

Bringing History Home

Dear Jud,

Who asked me almost 50 years ago — to please underline his misspelling + to date my newspaper clippings. Some profound lesson there — you came from such a great family. The Crawfords have had a huge, enduring impact on me. Let's keep that history going. Best, [Bill]

Bringing History Home

A Classroom Teacher's Quest to Make the Past Matter

Bill Schechter

ROWMAN & LITTLEFIELD
Lanham • Boulder • New York • London

Published by Rowman & Littlefield
A wholly owned subsidiary of The Rowman & Littlefield Publishing Group, Inc.
4501 Forbes Boulevard, Suite 200, Lanham, Maryland 20706
www.rowman.com

Unit A, Whitacre Mews, 26-34 Stannary Street, London SE11 4AB

British Library Cataloguing in Publication Information Available

Library of Congress Cataloging-in-Publication Data
Names: Schechter, Bill, author.
Title: Bringing history home : a classroom teacher's quest to make the past matter / Bill Schechter.
Description: Lanham : Rowman & Littlefield, an imprint of The Rowman & Littlefield Publishing Group, Inc., [2018] | Includes bibliographical references.
Identifiers: LCCN 2018035874| ISBN 9781475846638 (cloth : alk. paper) | ISBN 9781475846645 (pbk. : alk. paper) | ISBN 9781475846652 (electronic)
Subjects: LCSH: United States--History--Study and teaching (Secondary) | History--Study and teaching (Secondary)
Classification: LCC E175.8 .S364 2018 | DDC 973.071/2--dc23 LC record available at https://lccn.loc.gov/2018035874

∞ ™ The paper used in this publication meets the minimum requirements of American National Standard for Information Sciences Permanence of Paper for Printed Library Materials, ANSI/NISO Z39.48-1992.

Printed in the United States of America

For my family:

Sandy Shea and our sons Ethan and Jamie Schechter, my parents, Ruth and Jerry Schechter, and my grandparents, Max and Bessie Schechter and Sarah Karish, and my daughters-in-law, Stacy Drucker and Leakhena Schechter,

How fortunate I have been to be a part of your history.

And for the newest member of the clan, my grandson Lincoln Pierce Schechter,

How wonderful to be part of your future!

Consider what stuff history is made of, that for the most part it is merely a story agreed on by posterity. . . . I believe that, if I were to live the life of mankind over again myself, (which I would not be hired to do,) with the Universal History in my hands, I should not be able to tell what was what.

—Henry D. Thoreau, *Cape Cod*

The Past—the dark unfathom'd retrospect!
The teeming gulf, the sleepers and the shadows
The past! The infinite greatness of the past!
For what is the present after all, but a growth out of the past.

—Walt Whitman, *Leaves of Grass*

The past is never dead. It's not even past.

—William Faulkner, *Requiem for a Nun*

Unless you feel a thing, you can never guess its meaning.

—Emma Goldman, *Correspondence with Alexander Berkman*

Contents

Acknowledgments xi

Introduction 1

Prologue: It Was Only the First Day of School 5

1 Beginnings: What Helps Make a History Class Compelling? 9

2 Let There Be Music: Singing Our Way Through Trials and Tribulations 17

3 Theater in the Square: The Power of Make-Believe in the Classroom 29

4 Field Trips On My Mind: Taking It On the Road 37

5 History Begins At Home: Is It Knocking On *Your* Door? 49

6 Taking History Into the Hallways: Seed-Time of an Epiphany 59

7 Joining Hands to Minds: Building a Cabin for a Courtyard 75

8 Awakening the Muse: "Here Once the Embattled Farmers Stood" 83

9 Rummaging Through the Attic Trunk: A Few Other Odds and Ends Used to Bind Students to History 101

10 Getting Caught in History's Web: Students, Your Family Saga Is Before You 109

11 History in the Headlines: Why Newspapers Are a Teacher's Best Friend 117

12 Welcome to the Classroom World: Please Take a Seat 127

13 Bias Buzzing Around My Head: The "No-See-Ums" of the
     History Classroom   139

14 Charting a Course: One Way to Develop History Units   145

15 Not Just Civics Class, But a Civic Life: Democracy Makes Its
     Demands   159

Epilogue: Actually, There Is No Ending   167

Coda   171

About the Author   173

Acknowledgments

Books too have a history.

Foremost, I want to thank my family, without whose support my teaching career and hence this book would not have happened. My wife Sandy Shea and my sons Ethan and Jamie put up with a lot during those countless evenings and weekends of lesson planning, activity organizing, and grading. And without Sandy, this book project would never have been completed. She believed in it, encouraged and challenged me—whatever was needed. I won't even mention her editing and proofreading. No job too big or small.

My late parents, Ruth and Jerry Schechter, and my late brother, Danny Schechter, were part of this book's long foreground. Actually, they were the foreground. We were the children and grandchildren of immigrants and believed in the promise of American ideals. My parents and brother showed me that a hospital secretary could become a poet, a garment cutter a sculptor, and a high school editor an internationally known journalist. Their lives inspired me.

In the here and now, I want to thank friends Larry Aaronson, Leslie Cohen, Steve Cohen, Robin Espinola, Lucy Marx, and Dan Peppercorn for their ideas and support. I am also indebted to Fletcher Boland for his assistance with the *BringingHistoryHome* web page.

If it takes a village to raise a child, it takes a school—actually several schools—to make a teacher. I was a public school kid and proud of it. So thank you to my teachers at P.S. 95 in the Bronx who started me off and nurtured my interest in social studies. Thank you to Lou Simon and David Fuchs, my teachers at DeWitt Clinton High School. Did they think they were only teaching English and history? Please, they *were* the lesson. Thank you to Professor Gerd Korman for guiding me over the terrain of American social history at Cornell.

How can I even begin to acknowledge the support and example provided by my dedicated colleagues at Lincoln-Sudbury Regional High School in Sudbury, Massachusetts? They were commitment writ large, so enthusiastic about their subjects, so devoted to their students, and so selfless in their contributions to the Lincoln-Sudbury community. We were all fortunate to work at a school that accorded us freedom and respect—in short, a brave school. Much gratitude is owed to the late Jo Crawford and to Susan Frommer, Don Gould, Caroline Han, Paul Mitchell, Joe Pacenka, John Ritchie, Brad Sargent, Karen Sirkin, Thom Thacker, and Dani Weisse for helping me to grow as an educator in the broadest sense of that word.

Finally, thanks to the students of Lincoln-Sudbury who pushed me to become a better teacher. Their honesty, enthusiasm, skepticism, and curiosity drew me more deeply into history and made me more determined to find ways to share what I learned. They were always deserving of my best efforts and never became impatient when I repeated William Faulkner's words for the umpteenth time, "The past is never dead. It's not even past." Were truer words ever said?

All those acknowledged here contributed to whatever is useful in this book. For the book's limitations, I take the rap and am not embarrassed to admit I was still trying to figure out the art of teaching when the clock ran out.

ILLUSTRATIONS

Many of the projects mentioned in this book can be brought to life in living color through photographs. For those interested, chapter-by-chapter illustrations can be found at: www.BringingHistoryHome.com

CREDITS

I am grateful to those who gave permission to reprint excerpts from the following songs and poems.

Songs

"Brother, Can You Spare a Dime?" Lyrics by Yip Harburg
"Amoskeag Mill," Copyright 1996 Charlie Ball

Poems

"Questions of a Worker Who Reads," originally published in German in 1936 as "Fragen eines Lesenden Arbeiters," translated by Thomas Mark Kuhn. Copyright 1961, 1976 by Bertolt Brecht, translated by Thomas Mark Kuhn and David J. Constantine. Used by permission of Liveright Publishing Coproration.
"The Negro Mother," Reprinted by permission of Harold Ober Associates Incorporated. Copyright 1994 by the Langston Hughes Estate.
"The Negro Speaks of Rivers," Reprinted by permission of Harold Ober Associates Incorporated. Copyright 1994 by the Langston Hughes Estate.

Introduction

This is a book of ideas, suggestions, and advice for those who teach or aspire to teach high school history. That it was written at a challenging time for public education and for our nation's teachers hardly needs stating. Most of them are underpaid, increasingly disempowered in their schools, and often treated like functionaries rather than professionals.

Not surprisingly, teacher turnover has become a persistent problem for school districts, with almost half of new teachers leaving after just five years. This churn—as well as the early departure of more experienced staff—adds billions of dollars in recruiting and training costs to school districts across the country. Worse yet, uncertified teachers often fill the gap, which is certainly not fair to students. The extent and impact of this teacher attrition problem has been the subject of rigorous studies at both the University of Pennsylvania and Stanford.

There are several causes for this worrisome state of affairs. Inadequate state revenues have placed school budgets under pressure, causing teacher compensation to fall even further behind that of other college graduates. The roiling teacher protests and strikes in West Virginia, Kentucky, and Oklahoma in 2018 speak to this profound dissatisfaction.

Teacher morale and career longevity have also been negatively affected by the standardized testing assessment protocols implemented nationwide since the 1990s. Heralded as a means of raising academic standards by holding both students and teachers accountable, the use of high-stakes standardized tests has generated considerable controversy. But whatever one thinks of the effectiveness and validity of such exams, supporters and critics would probably agree that these assessment instruments have diminished teacher autonomy in the classroom and imposed more centralized control over curriculum.

Whether an education based on standardized tests can produce the kind of schooling parents want for their children will ultimately be determined by their voices and votes. This book argues—through example and lived experience—that there is a better, more enduring way to encourage students to learn and, more importantly, to make them *want* to learn.

Teachers must have the creative freedom to experiment with the kind of pedagogy and curriculum that can make education an intellectual and experiential adventure. The famed Concordian Henry David Thoreau reminds us that "in the long run men only hit what they aim at. Therefore, though they should fail immediately, they had better aim at something high." In that spirit, all of us—teachers, administrators, legislators, and parents—should aim high and try to inspire a lifelong love of learning. Reducing education to test prep sets a low standard and will not serve students well in their lives after high school.

But will underpaid teachers be willing to put in the work required to re-imagine education and pursue their classroom visions? To realize the dreams and ideals that first motivated them to take education classes? The answer is "Yes" if they are treated like professionals and given an opportunity to actively participate in departmental and school-wide decision making. Respect and participation are the foundation stones of commitment.

The suggestions offered in these pages arise from my three decades of experience as a history teacher at Lincoln-Sudbury Regional High School in Sudbury, Massachusetts. The respect and relative freedom accorded the faculty there encouraged teachers to go well beyond what the union contract required. This is because we felt less like employees and more like valued members of an educational community. That made all the difference in our careers.

In the first chapter of *Bringing History Home*, I make the case for the importance of studying the discipline and the reasons why it presents an inherently engrossing challenge. The next ten chapters discuss various pedagogical approaches, curricula, and resources that can help bring history—and history classes—alive. This includes the use of music, poetry, field trips, simulations, and newspapers and also ways to strengthen a history program by taking it into the hallways and the life of a school.

In chapter 12, "Welcome to the Classroom World," the issue of organizing physical space is discussed, as well as a teacher's way of being in the classroom. Reading materials, assignments, and discipline are also addressed. Chapter 13 is devoted to an extended discussion of bias, a nettlesome challenge for all history teachers, particularly in these polarized times.

Although there are many ways to prepare and organize units, chapter 14, "Charting a Course," describes one teacher's way of getting under the hood and dealing with the nuts and bolts. As critical as curriculum design is in creating an effective and memorable history class, explaining the process of how to *actually* do it sometimes gets slighted in teacher-training programs.

The last chapter focuses on a closely related subject, civics, and why teaching the Constitution is just the beginning, not the end, of preparing young people for a civic life in a democratic society.

Woven through any teacher's reflections about education, there are the students—the very reason we show up in the classroom every day. They are growing up today under extraordinary pressures in school and out. Every September, despite all, they look to the future with bright hope.

In his poem "An Old Man's Thought of School," Walt Whitman described how he viewed the students as their public schools fitted them out for a great journey.

> And these I see—these sparkling eyes,
> These stores of mystic meaning—these young lives,
> Building, equipping, like a fleet of ships—immortal ships!
> Soon to sail over measureless seas,
> On the Soul's voyage.

If we can look out on our classes and see what he did, the sight will buoy us even on the stormiest days.

Prologue

It Was Only the First Day of School

Students help us to become better teachers, and so what if their lessons are not always intentional or delivered in a kind way? The "instruction" usually doesn't begin on the first day, but there was one memorable September lesson given by a student who refused to follow simple directions.

The exact year this occurred has been lost to time, but it can be said with confidence it actually did happen on one of the thirty-five first days of school in this teacher's career. Though the year's formidable mountain of historical material loomed before us, it always seemed a good idea to first take some time to help the kids get to know each other and feel comfortable in their new class. After all, comfort and active participation often go hand-in-hand.

We began with a "getting-to-know-you" exercise that involved students introducing themselves and sharing the name of one of their heroes. This exercise had only two rules: (1) The hero chosen had to be a historical personage, not a family member, and (2) Students had to briefly explain why they made the choice they did. One sentence was sufficient.

About half the students in this sophomore class had taken their turns, offering up valid but mostly predictable choices (George Washington, Susan B. Anthony, Abraham Lincoln, Martin Luther King, etc.), when it was "Megan's" turn.

She introduced herself and then said, "My hero is my uncle." This elicited a friendly chuckle from the front of the room, a reminder about the rule, and this helpful prompt: "Anyone else . . . you know . . . some historical figure?"

But again she said, "My uncle." "Ah, your uncle," came the response, "but anyone else?" "My uncle," she repeated for a third time. She wasn't blinking or smiling but was staring directly at the person trying to prod her.

No educator wants to embarrass a student, least of all on the first day of school. Moreover, there might have been a cognitive or developmental issue involved here. She was probably doing the best she could. With a touch of condescension, a surrender statement was proffered: "Okay, so please tell us why your uncle is your hero? He must be an amazing guy."

She turned and pointed to a poster hanging on the classroom wall and said, "My uncle is lying under that woman who is screaming." The poster depicted an enlargement of the Pulitzer Prize–winning photo of the young woman who first came to the aid of one of the students fatally wounded at Kent State in 1970. It turns out that fatally wounded man was her uncle.

It was one of those heart-stopping classroom moments a teacher never forgets. The plan was for a friendly, low-key, ice-breaking exercise that would give students a chance to speak up on this first day and hear their own voice as part of a larger classroom community.

The lesson turned out, well, differently because one girl decided not to follow her teacher's rules. She spoke. Then silence. Stone silence. The very last thing anyone expected was for history itself to actually intrude into this history class, the full weight and awful burden of it, the unexpected living fact of a student lying dead at Kent State. Somehow, someway, a decade or so later, one of his nieces came to be sitting in my classroom. From nowhere a spark suddenly arced between these two dates. The chastened and stunned teacher barely managed to speak the words "Thank you for sharing that, Megan."

The lesson was well taught and valuable. Her response conveyed an important reminder that our students do not arrive in the history class as free-floating bits of cosmic dust. They cross the classroom threshold pulled and pushed by their own personal comet's worth of history. The father who served in Vietnam and returned with a knapsack full of poetry. The parents who protested for civil rights or against war. The grandmother who worked alongside Rosie the Riveter. The relatives who fled the terror of the South or who stood in breadlines and survived the Great Depression or were interned in a camp or were persecuted by McCarthy.

Then there are great-grandparents, those who brought the family over from Russia, Ireland, or Italy and bequeathed their names and legacy to our students, the O'Briens, Levines, Martinellis, Smiths, and Adamses. The ancestors who were enslaved on cotton plantations in Alabama or worked long hours in the textile mills of Lowell. These specters shadowed my students.

It's September. The kids sit upright in their chairs filled with the shiny hope that a new school year always brings. Whether realizing it or not, they are not present to study a subject outside of themselves. There is no distance here. Their families have already been walking their own chosen or chance or imposed path through history. They are, possibly, victims, survivors, beneficiaries, participants, or stakeholders in the stories they will study. Perhaps all of the above. Their families helped make the history they will study this year.

Historians work tirelessly to document and connect facts. Students are already inextricably connected to that web. A good history course will try to help them to understand just how they are connected and what the significance is for themselves and for the subject they are studying.

"My hero is my uncle."

Chapter One

Beginnings

What Helps Make a History Class Compelling?

I was a wretched history student. History classes were like visits to the wax-works or the Region of the Dead. The past was lifeless, hollow, dumb. They taught us about the past so that we should resign ourselves with drained con-sciences to the present: not to make history, which was already made, but to accept it. Poor history had stopped breathing: betrayed in academic texts, lied about in classrooms, drowned in dates, they had imprisoned her in museums, and buried her, with floral wreaths, beneath statuary bronze and monumental marble.

—Eduardo Galeano, *Memory of Fire*

Those who labor in the vineyards of high school history classrooms know it can be a hard job. In fact, according to a 2004 Gallup survey, history is the least favorite major subject among students. In such a present-oriented soci-ety, the challenges for history teachers are large and the encouraging words of the playwright Samuel Beckett more than welcome: "Ever tried. Ever failed. No matter. Try Again. Fail again. Fail better."

But history teachers need hardly settle for "fail better." Hopefully, some of what's described here—including the failures, of which there were quite a few in a long career—may help others wake the dead in the mausoleum of the past. The various resources, experiments, and activities discussed in these pages were one teacher's attempt to make history present, to invite students into it, and to surround them with it.

A great debt is owed to my own public school teachers and to the colleagues who later provided inspiration and generously shared their curriculum. Each of the ideas that follow is a template with a thousand variations. Walt Whitman put it best when he said of *Leaves of Grass*, "The words of my book nothing, the drift of them everything." Hopefully, other teachers will find some helpful drift here.

Many students really don't understand why they study history, only that they are required to do so. For too many, history is a journey through a dense, dark forest of facts they are called upon to map, navigate, and memorize. Why these facts and not others? That question is way above their pay grade. Their assigned job is to "learn," not to question *why*.

Of course there is value in learning facts, especially in our brave new world of so-called fake news. Facts give us a solid ground to stand on in a universe where the law of gravity sometimes seems on the verge of being repealed. Clearly, history classes without facts or content are pointless. Besides, many skills are taught when students "learn" facts: the process of absorbing and retaining material, organizing it, reasoning out causation and chronology, and so on. Facts are obviously essential in developing a basic literacy about our country's past. But only that often unasked or ignored question—"Why?"—can open the door to the mysteries of the past. As Virgil tells us, *Felix, qui potuit rerum cognoscere causas* [Fortunate are those who know the causes of things].

The challenges facing history teachers are formidable. Five years out of high school, or less, most of your students will not remember what the Treaty of Guadalupe Hidalgo is. You taught it. You tested it. They studied it. They knew it on the test. Then . . . *boom* . . . they forgot it. Even worse, most of our students will betray us in college by choosing to major in a completely different subject.

Worst of all, that familiar chestnut often used to justify historical study, namely, that by studying the lessons of history we can avoid the mistakes of the past, is very problematic. After getting stuck in the Big Muddy of Vietnam, we managed to find ourselves half-buried in other intractable conflicts. The lessons of the Great Depression did not, regrettably, prevent the economic collapse of 2008.

So why should history teachers even bother trying? What do we hope to achieve in our classes? What enduring impact can educators have who are charged with teaching about the past? What can we realistically do?

To begin with, we should not park students in front of computers, or subject them to continuous PowerPoint presentations that are little more than digital worksheets, or disperse them to endless group work. Only the human connection that teachers can forge with their classes, and students with each other, can help bring history to life. Certainly, discussion, debates, group work, even stodgy textbooks can have an important role to play in every class. But when was the last time a graduate returned to tell an old teacher how unforgettable a textbook passage was?

An influential teacher can never be a mere coach or "facilitator." The teacher's role is to inspire and to model clear thinking, good writing, and habits of mind; to create a space and opportunity for free and active inquiry; to pose questions that generate intellectual tension and curiosity; and to share his or her knowledge of the past.

To do these things, a teacher has to enter the classroom daily with a briefcase full of enthusiasm, a deep personal interest in the subject, a familiarity with the material, a plan for teaching it, and lots of good stories. History, after all, is the biggest story of all. Teachers have to "keep it real," and this starts when they themselves believe that studying the past is urgently important.

Here are two stories that illustrate what can make learning memorable. The first involves an English class one-half century ago at DeWitt Clinton High School in the Bronx. The English teacher who plays the starring role in this memory got a little carried away while reading aloud a passage from *Hamlet* and stepped into the garbage can. After the mishap, he tried to make an incisive point about the play, a point that unfortunately has gone missing from this author's memory. However, the image of his foot in the trash has remained sharply engraved for five decades.

What also made a lasting impression on his students was his obvious love for Shakespeare, which has sent many of us back to the plays from time to time in search of the source of his passion and to rediscover the Bard for ourselves. The lesson turned out to be the teacher.

The other story is about the day a certain ninth grader came home from school bursting with excitement about a lesson in English class: "Dad, did you know novels can have more than one meaning?" It was as if a window had opened in his mind to reveal a whole new world.

There is also a closed window high up in most students' mental attic labeled "History." It too must be thrown open. Through it, they will more clearly see one of the few incontestable facts they will ever encounter: that what we call history is itself an interpretation, culled from the great ocean of the past by historians with different perspectives, prejudices, values, conceptual frameworks, political allegiances, and patterns of logical inference. Yes, we can all agree that George Washington was born on February 22, but the meaning of Washington's life—the general, the president, the slave-owner—is subject to widely varying views.

To understand the exciting challenge that history presents, students must become conversant with concepts that will enable them to distinguish between the paired concepts "fact and truth," "bias and objectivity," "opinion and interpretation." At the very beginning of their year's study, they need to consider the words that Charles Dickens puts into the mouth of his character Mr. Gradgrind in *Hard Times*: "Now, what I want is, Facts. Teach these boys and girls nothing but Facts. Facts alone are wanted in life."

And then they need to compare these words to those of the American historian Howard Zinn, who reminds us in *A People's History of the United States* that even fact-filled textbooks have a bias:

> [There] is no such thing as a pure fact, innocent of interpretation. Behind every fact presented to the world—by a teacher, a writer, anyone—is a judgment. The judgment that has been made is that this fact is important, and that other facts, omitted, are not important.

They need to understand what Bertolt Brecht was getting at in his poem *Questions of a Worker Who Reads*:

> Who built the seven gates of Thebes?
> In books you will read the names of kings.
> Was it the kings who dragged the stones into place?

They need an opportunity to discuss whether Norman Mailer was correct when he said, "People move forward into the future out of the way they comprehend the past" or what Harry Truman was getting at when he said, "There is nothing new in the world except the history you don't know." They need to decide if they agree with Ken Kesey that "the past is funny . . . it never seems to let things lie, finished, it never seems to stay in place as it should" or with William Faulkner when he said, "The past is never dead. It's not even past."

Of course, students need to understand how to take notes, do research, write well, and avoid the pitfalls of historical fallacies. They need to know content. But they also require a historiographical foundation that enables them to see history for what it is: a problem, an argument, and not merely a timeline and list of terms and names. It's in that understanding that the beating heart of history can be found.

They will be able to feel that heartbeat when they read conflicting interpretations of the same topic and are able to drill down deeply enough to discover where, why, and how the historians disagree—and the significance of those disagreements.

Students will come to appreciate that that truth requires not memorization but evidence reasoned to a convincing conclusion; not "offhand" opinions but research and logic. To be admitted to the arena of continuing debate, students will need to bring a ticket punched with knowledge, critical thinking skills, the power of analysis, and the capacity to express themselves clearly.

Something happened here. What was it? Why did it happen? Do all agree? What can we make of the diverse narratives? Why should we care?

These are some of the thoughts that should be humming and thrumming through the minds of our students as we move from September to June.

If only history were as simple as those prefabricated standardized tests with their choice of "a, b, c, or all of the above." If only memorization and regurgitation could pass for education, we would never be burdened by the troubling question of who decides what facts appear on the exam. How are they plucked from the myriad of facts in the Milky Way of the past? Isn't the ostensibly objective test itself an interpretation of an interpretation?

The sad fate of the Treaty of Guadalupe Hidalgo in our collective memory should not cause us to despair. Students and graduates can always look it up. The good news is that the basic historiographical concepts presented in an introductory unit will keep surfacing throughout the academic year. Students may forget this fact or that (or even both this *and* that), but they will never forget this slippery, sliding, twisting, turning trail of the thing we call history.

The complexity of the past must be placed before students so they can understand the challenges of pursuing the truth and not just memorizing what truths they are given. History classes must involve a steep mental climb. Facts must be found and unavoidable arguments over meaning engaged. Which pathway in the dark forest will best lead to the truth we seek? That's the question that should animate history students.

History teachers know the content they teach has great power, replete with stories no literature class can possibly match. You want characters? You want suspense, plot twists, unlikely resolutions, drama, heroism, villainy, victory against the greatest odds, defeat in the noblest of causes? This "cast of thousands" story can stir a child's imagination, so why should a teacher ever retreat to the thin gruel of social studies stew? Students must be led back into the past on an extended field trip that will move, excite, intrigue, and perplex them much like it did our great national poet Walt Whitman in *Leaves of Grass*.

When I Read the Book

When I read the book, the biography famous,
And is this then (said I) what the author calls a man's life?
And so will some one when I am dead and gone write my life?
(As if any man really knew aught my life,
Why even I myself I often think know little or nothing of my real life,
Only a few hints, a few diffused faint clews and indirections
I seek for my own use to trace out here.)

With Whitman's note of caution in mind, it is time to throw open that attic window and invite our students into the argument that constitutes history. There is truth hidden there if we have the persistence to find it. And if our attempts to reconcile different perspectives don't reveal the truth we seek, it won't be for lack of critical thinking, weighing, pondering, and ruminating. Let's give it a shot.

The stakes are as great as the challenges. We are teaching young people in a democratic society that requires literate citizens with an understanding of how our world and country came to be and the ability to place current controversies into a larger context. Citizens in turn need to believe they can participate in history, to feel empowered by the same sense of possibility that motivated heroic figures and social movements to struggle for a "more perfect union."

We must also try to remember the story of the "losers" and victims whose suffering is also part of the American experience. They bequeath to us their courage and their hopes. Besides, as Bob Dylan reminds us, "The loser now will be later to win." Maybe.

Finally, we all need history to answer that timeless personal question "*Who am I?*"—a process that often begins by first understanding how our grandparents and parents shaped us while traveling their own hard road. We are products of that history. This epic is *our* story.

The greatest challenge is to teach our citizen-students in a way that instills a lifelong interest in history even after they commit heresy and choose to become artists, engineers, doctors and nurses, factory workers, or waitresses. Whether we succeed or not depends on many factors, including the depth of our knowledge, the intensity of our passion, our ability to make a personal connection to our students, and of course the pedagogy we use to draw students into the material. Even the meeting time of the class can play its bit part. How about a senior class at 8 a.m. or right after lunch? Yikes.

Despite all the challenges, something can come alive in a classroom, and it has nothing to do with worksheets, test prep, or the endless loop of mind-numbing PowerPoint presentations that this retired teacher later observed as a practicum supervisor at a variety of high schools.

Success will not always crown a teacher's efforts. There will be tired times of year, solid weeks of rain, and lesson plans that fall flat. Still these pages may provide a glimpse—perhaps a reminder—of what's possible when teachers are given the academic freedom to be creative, to shape their curriculum, to enjoy substantial autonomy in the classroom, and to participate in the life of a school.

You will find no lesson plans in this book, rather a collage of ideas, activities, and strategies to rouse the past and bring it home for today's high school students. Inevitably, these pages will echo with a teacher's memories of the planned and the unexpected, the spontaneous and the serendipitous.

Sometimes there was magic.

Chapter Two

Let There Be Music

Singing Our Way Through Trials and Tribulations

A fact stated barely is dry. It must be the vehicle of some humanity in order to be of interest to us. It is like giving a man a stone when he asks you for bread.
— Henry D. Thoreau, *Journal*, February 23, 1860

Using music in the classroom can help a teacher "wake" history, so it's best to never pass up a good song. But how exactly does it help? We'll get to that. But before striking up the band (or more accurately turning on Spotify or the CD player), there's some important context to consider.

In the long winding history of American education, there's been only one constant: the notion that the newest idea (or often a recycled idea passing as brand-new) is not only the *best* idea, but the *only* idea. It would be difficult to list all the panaceas that have come down the pike just in the last two decades without re-creating the old Manhattan phonebook.

When one of these "best" ideas makes its debut, it usually arrives with a great amount of fanfare, if not the force of a revelation. One almost expects it was carried down from Mt. Sinai by Moses himself. But, unfortunately, too many school leaders forsake a more deliberate consideration in favor of a lurching toward the latest and greatest. Yesterday's truth becomes, well, just so yesterday.

The reason we keep swinging on this pendulum is simple: educators are eager for a miracle cure for classroom boredom, that one approach that will electrify struggling or uninterested students into a state of permanent excitement. We also want to close the achievement gap so that all schools can

become exemplars of equal educational opportunity regardless of how un-
equal our society might remain. We'd prefer to have our cake and to eat it
too.

The buzzwords change but the buzz keeps buzzing. Nowadays we hear a
lot about "personalized learning," "individualized instruction," "data-driven
instruction," "online learning," "project-based learning," and "differentiated
instruction." Each of these ideas doubtless has something to offer to a classroom of learners. The problem starts (or repeats) when each respectively
becomes "the one best idea" and the cause of education reform becomes
tethered to the most recent pedagogy *du jour*.

The cost or collateral damage can be the destruction of a classroom's
interactive potential, its culture if you will, as students are dispersed to the far
corners of a classroom for a year's worth of personalized-individualized-
differentiated project-based learning or what-have-you.

But there's an abiding truth that never changes in schools: transformative
education is a *human* enterprise. It's about teachers and students working,
studying, learning, and laughing together. Take away that human element
and the academic equivalent of the trackless Sahara stretches endlessly before you.

Thoreau, whose journal entry introduced this chapter, begins his most
celebrated nature essay *Walking* by stating that he wished "to say a word for
Nature." Perhaps it's time to say a word on behalf of another ecosystem: the
"whole classroom" and the interactive energy that a class can generate *together*. Most of the time we do not need computers because we've got us. So
here is to the "whole classroom" approach!

Now, why the singing?

Imagine a hand-printed quotation on a battered piece of manila folder
hanging above the chalkboard in a classroom in Sudbury, Massachusetts. The
words on it are attributed to the anarchist Emma Goldman: "Unless you feel
a thing, you can never guess its meaning." Those eleven words have profound implications for the teaching of history. They certainly did for the
teacher in that classroom.

Yes, it *is* critical for students to "know" the facts, and equally important
for them to try, however tentatively, to search for meaning. But if Goldman is
right and "feeling the thing" is essential to understanding, then teachers must
provide students with a variety of materials—primary documents, poems,
films, interviews, etc.—in which a faint heartbeat can be detected. This will
help to get some blood pumping through that dry viscera of facts.

Songs can help animate the history classroom. Through lyric and melody, they present a concert's worth of subjective and emotional perspective on events. In them we hear the voiceprints of the past, the tone and texture of a period, the experiences of the people who lived through those times and their personal take on contentious issues.

Of course, only part of a song's essence can be divined by reading the words. Unlike other kinds of source documents, a song's meaning can only be fully expressed when it takes flight through singing. It's then that the feeling of it is expressed. And there is a bonus. Singing illustrates the power that an inclusive, unfragmented classroom can have in drawing students together into a common pursuit of understanding.

Here is how the musical experience may well unfold in your classroom. Within the first few weeks of the school year, inform your students you are going to sing a song together, and have the song cued up and ready to go. The students will be like, *Wha? A song? We have to sing?*

Depending on the personalities involved and the class chemistry, expect the first attempt to be very weak. The kids will feel embarrassed. And the songs will be so uncool, not only not current, but perhaps even a moldy century old. Meanwhile, the teacher must ask the students to turn up their volume knobs. Sometimes they can be goaded or kidded into putting a little more heart into it. Alas, mostly they will continue to sit ramrod straight at their desks mouthing the lyrics on the handout with precious little sound coming out.

Now is the time for extreme measures. Ask everyone to come down into "the pit"—the area between their desks and yours. Lounging on the floor, packed together, but without having to look at each other directly, they will do much better. The act of singing together helps bond these new classmates, and friendship and good feeling slowly begin to replace self-consciousness. The value of collective singing for group building makes music a gift that keeps on giving.

Initially, they may have joined in song for the novelty and fun of it. Then students begin to listen to the songs and absorb all they are imparting. Sometimes, and sooner than seemed possible, the class will find itself lifted up and carried away. It is as if this planned and contrived exercise has passed through a chrysalis and metamorphoses into something real.

Admittedly—and this insight has been personally field-tested!—it's a great advantage when using music in the classroom if the teacher's voice isn't good enough to intimidate the students.

Now, what kind of songs?

In *Leaves of Grass*, Walt Whitman celebrated the pervasive presence of music in our everyday lives:

> I HEAR America singing, the varied carols I hear;
> Those of mechanics—each one singing his, as it should be, blithe and strong;
> The carpenter singing his, as he measures his plank or beam . . .
>
> . . . .
>
> The delicious singing of the mother—or of the young wife at work—or of the
> girl sewing or washing—Each singing what belongs to her, and to none else;
> The day what belongs to the day—At night, the party of young fellows, robust,
> friendly,
> Singing, with open mouths, their strong melodious songs.

In the Twentieth Century and Postwar America courses, students joined in singing the songs of enslaved people, early millworkers and miners, union activists, suffragists, political party campaigners, dust bowl refugees, lonely World War II home-front lovers, civil rights freedom fighters, teenagers, doo-woppers, and hippies. The songs created the soundscape of the story they were journeying through in the classroom and helped illuminate a country in constant motion and a people striving for a better life.

Occasionally, atmospherics helped add another dimension of feeling. For example, when we were listening to the jazz that inspired the Beat writers, most of the lights were turned off except for one red bulb before students were asked to read aloud Ginsberg's famous poem *America*—or their own versions of it.

Beyond sound, melody, tone, and texture, the songs provide important content and context to units of study. Here is just a brief sampling of the many songs sung.

Slavery

Auction Block

> No more auction block for me
> No more, no more
> No more auction block for me
> Many thousand gone
> No more peck of corn for me

. . . No more driver's lash for me
. . . No more pint of salt for me . . .

Industrialization

Hard Times Cotton Mill Girls

I worked in the cotton mill all my life,
I ain't got nothin' but a Barlow knife.
Hard times cotton mill girls,
Hard times everywhere.
And it's hard times cotton mill girls,
Hard times cotton mill girls,
Hard times cotton mill girls,
. . .
Us kids worked twelve hours a day
For fourteen cents of measly pay
Hard times, cotton mill girls,
Hard times everywhere . . .

Bread & Roses

As we go marching, marching
In the beauty of the day
A million darkened kitchens
A thousand mill lofts grey
Are touched with all the radiance
That a sudden sun discloses
For the people hear us singing
Bread and roses, bread and roses

As we go marching, marching
We battle too for men
For they are women's children
And we mother them again
Our lives shall not be sweetened
From birth until life closes
Hearts starve as well as bodies
Give us bread, but give us roses . . .

Populism

The Farmer Is the Man

When the farmer comes to town with his wagon broken down
The farmer is the man that feeds 'em all
If you'll only look an' see, I think you will agree
That the farmer is the man that feeds 'em all
The farmer is the man
The farmer is the man
Lives on credit 'til the fall
Then they take him by the hand
And they lead him from the land
And the middle man's the one that gets it all
When the lawyer hangs around, and the butcher cuts a pound
The farmer is the man that feeds 'em all
And the preacher and the cook, they go strollin' by the brook
But the farmer is the man that feeds 'em all . . .

The Great Depression

Brother, Can You Spare a Dime?

They used to tell me I was building a dream
And so I followed the mob
When there was earth to plow or guns to bear
I was always there right on the job

They used to tell me I was building a dream
With peace and glory ahead
Why should I be standing in line
Just wait for bread?

Once I built a railroad, I made it run
Made it race against time
Once I built a railroad, now it's done
Brother, can you spare a dime . . .

Slave spirituals and folk songs. Hymns. Campaign ditties. Songs of hardship and struggle. Jazz and Tin Pan Alley's popular music of the Twenties and Thirties. From the depths of the Great Depression, the soundscape of American history wound on to the titanic struggles of a World War with its big bands and sentimental ballads like "I'll Be Seeing You" and "It's Been a

Long, Long Time" then on to the Fifties where a new generation called "teenagers" scandalously began to "Rock Around the Clock."

This musical trail continued through the tumultuous Sixties when young people found a new catechism in songs like "Teach Your Children Well" and linked arms while singing powerful anthems of hope.

> We shall overcome
> We shall overcome
> We shall overcome, some day.
> Oh, deep in my heart,
> I do believe We shall overcome, some day.
>
> We'll walk hand in hand,
> We'll walk hand in hand,
> We'll walk hand in hand, some day.
> Oh, deep in my heart, I do believe
> We shall overcome, some day.

. . . before heading into the disco clubs of the Seventies to lose themselves in the infectious rhythm of the Bee Gees' "Staying Alive." Meanwhile, in the Eighties, somewhere in the Bronx, rap with its driving beat, twisting rhymes, and wordplay was waiting to explode with the anger, frustration, and aspirations of those condemned to the racism and poverty of our inner cities.

These songs and hundreds more both expressed and shaped the *zeitgeist* of their respective periods. They invite us into the emotional truths of eras our students may have read about but still seem as distant to them as ancient history. Through lyrics and melodies, the past "speaks" again. And unlike today's text messages that also compel our attention, only songs leave us humming.

In addition to reinforcing factual narrative, music can catalyze discussions, debates, and role-playing. Songs restore history to the people who made it and to the students later required to study it. They help to bring history home.

Songs make classes memorable—literally. One student wrote in an evaluation, "At first I giggled when our teacher asked us to sing along, but after a while I joined in with the class and began to feel the true power of the music." Another wrote that "the music we hear in class created a bridge between past and present . . . and made it possible for me to pull myself out of my own period, even if just for a moment." Recently, a student who had graduated a decade earlier after taking a World Crisis course, shared this memory: "I'll never forget when you walked into class—we were studying the 'Troubles' in Ireland—and had us sing a song by that Irish group, the Commitments."

Of course, the words that will mean the most to any teacher will come from a student with a request. "I just heard a song about Vietnam. Can I bring it in for the class to hear?" This happened.

In 2004, one song in particular led to a moving moment in a sophomore Twentieth Century class. The experience shows how hard it is to predict where a classroom lesson can take a teacher and class once the muse of serendipity takes over. It all began with a newly discovered contemporary mill song that seemed to be a worthy addition to the course's Industrialization playlist. Written by Charlie Ball and performed by a group called Plainfolk, it was called "Amoskeag Mill."

> Amoskeag Mill, your spirit has flown
> Shadows have lengthened and the weeds they have grown
> And the Merrimac River wanders lost and alone
> Amoskeag Mill, your spirit has flown
>
> Amoskeag Mill, weave us a tale
> Like you wove the wool skeins and the cottons in bale
> Our eyes they grow dim and our memories fail
> Amoskeag Mill, weave us a tale
>
> *Chorus:*
>
> Two miles long, half a mile wide
> Twenty-thousand men and women working inside
> Lived for their work and worked till they died
> Call it damn hard work, call it Amoskeag pride
> Let the sun beat down, let the wind blow chill
> But nothing stopped production at the Amoskeag Mill
> Call it Amoskeag luck or the good Lord's will
> But the looms kept running at the Amoskeag Mill.

September came around and suddenly a new Twentieth Century class took its seats. Now imagine something odd—a classroom filled with twenty-four boys and only three girls, rather than the more usual 50-50 split. Surprise! Demoralization! Having twenty-four immature sophomore boys in a class did not bode well for a singing year. There were too few girls to act mature for!

So much for judging too quickly. Teachers should be required to regularly write on the board "Do not stereotype students" a hundred times. This turned out to be a wonderful class, and that realization came during the very first unit when they heard the "Amoskeag Mill" song for the first time. In a kind of trial-by-fire of an entire year's musical truth, they grew quiet, listened to the song . . . and they loved it! They actually asked, "Can we sing it again . . . and *again*?"

Though the students sang many other songs that year, this first one would remain their favorite. It became what passed for a class theme song, with a last rendition just before school let out for summer vacation. But something even more unforgettable happened that year.

In February, a long obituary appeared in the *Boston Globe* that a parent happened to notice and thought the class might want to read. The headline memorialized a woman named Alice Olivier who as a teenager had labored in a textile mill and served as the sole support of her family of thirteen. Many decades later, in her sixties, she finally returned to school and became the valedictorian of her high school class. That was amazing enough, but what particularly caught the class's attention was that this woman had worked in New Hampshire's Amoskeag Mill, the very one featured in our wildly popular class chart-topper.

The obituary related an incredible life story that fairly leapt out of the history of American industrialization. Students were moved by the article because of the way it put a human face on so much of the history they had studied. They decided to make a recording of the class singing the Amoskeag song and send it to the bereaved family, whose general address had been noted in the obituary. The tape was accompanied by a photo of the class, looking solemnly at the camera, with two students holding a sign that read In Memory of Alice M. Olivier.

In Alice Olivier's life, the students had found a bridge connecting past to present, and they chose to walk across it. There was no response for many weeks. They wondered if the address was wrong. Or did the bereaved family think their offering was just plain weird? Finally, one day after they had nearly given up, an extraordinary letter arrived from one of Mrs. Oliver's daughters, Ellen Duclos. Like several others in her family, she had become a teacher. It turned out that the class's gesture had meant a great deal to them, as she explained in her letter to the school principal.

March 17, 2004
Dear Sir:

I am writing to tell you of a most wonderful and deeply moving experience which occurred a few weeks ago.

A large FedEx envelope, addressed to me, arrived from Lincoln-Sudbury Regional High School. Since I do not know anyone there, my curiosity was piqued. The envelope contained a letter from the 20th Century American History class. In this letter, the students identified themselves as sophomores who began their class this year by studying industrialization, which included reading about working conditions in old New England textile mills. Their teacher has evidently taught them many songs as another way to make history come alive. Their favorite song was one about the Amoskeag Mills.

I share all of this with you because sometime in February a parent had sent into this class the story which had appeared in the *Boston Globe* about my mother's death on January 31.

I live in Concord, NH and my mother died in a nursing home in the small town of Epsom, not far from my home. The *Globe* called me about expanding the obituary into a story after a reporter for the *Globe* read the lengthy obituary about my Mom in the *Lowell Sun*. We had placed it in that newspaper because my daughter-in-law's family all live in Lowell.

The class were attracted to the article because of the reference to the Amoskeag Mills. After reading the article, the students wrote to tell me that they believed my mother was an incredible woman—which she was—with an amazing story of courage and determination.

Included in the envelope was also a beautiful card, which all of the students in the class had signed, along with a picture of the students, several of whom were standing and holding a sign which reads, "In Memory of Alice M. Olivier."

There was more. They enclosed a tape recording of the class singing their favorite mill song, "The Amoskeag Mill," because, they wrote, it was "an expression of their sympathy for my family and respect for my mother, Mrs. Alice M. Olivier."

The letter closed by stating my mother "inspired" them "because even though her life presented great challenges, she always took them on and kept moving forward." One of my sons is a High School History teacher here in Concord, NH and when I shared all of this with him, he was impressed with all that this represents for both the students and their teacher.

I thought that you should be made aware of what a wonderful class of young people these sophomores are. As an educator myself, I'm aware of the influence which teachers have on students with whom they interact daily. [The teacher not only used songs] to raise his students' level of knowledge regarding industrialization and the enormous impact of the New England textile mills, but he personalized the facts which the class has studied by making each student aware of a woman, my mother, Alice M. Olivier, who died at the age of 88.

The story of this humble, unassuming, and very motivated woman is truly amazing. The kindness shown to me and my family by this sophomore, 20th Century American History class, as well as the respect for my mother, whom they would have loved if they'd had the opportunity to meet her, are memories I will treasure. The song, "Amoskeag Mill" which is on the tape they sent us, made me cry, as it resurrected the stories I heard so many times growing up. The stories of all the girls, boys, women and men who lived, worked and died in the shadow of the Amoskeag Mills.

Most Sincerely,
Elaine M. Duclos

The students were so touched and happy that their gesture had been appreciated. Of course, the teacher also found it gratifying that one educator understood what another had intended. But when a letter like this is received, history itself takes on a different meaning. How easy to forget that one person's history lesson is another's life. Was this a valuable experience? Would it have been better to more strictly budget classroom time in order to move more efficiently though the curriculum or the official state's history frameworks?

There is a lesson here for teachers everywhere. In the words of the old folk-music movement of the 1950s, "Lift Every Voice"—and, whenever possible, help set history to music.

Chapter Three

Theater in the Square

The Power of Make-Believe in the Classroom

> The stage is a magic circle where only the most real things happen, a neutral territory outside the jurisdiction of Fate where stars may be crossed with impunity. A truer and more real place does not exist in all the universe.
>
> —P. S. Baber, *Cassie Draws the Universe*

All the world's a stage—so why not the classroom? But with this difference: the audience will also need to be part of the cast.

Few activities can provide classes with more bang for the pedagogical buck than simulations. These exercises have the potential to place students directly inside the drama of history where they have to work through the same political conflicts and moral dilemmas faced by actual historical figures, be they the high and mighty or *hoi polloi*.

Additionally, these activities give students the opportunity to express their theatricality—call it legalized showing-off—and to bring the full range of human emotions into a classroom. Expressions of indignation, courage, confusion, cowardice, laughter (almost always real), and crying (almost always fake, except once) drifted across our stage. Shakespeare would have approved.

Sometimes the simulations can be brief. For example, when studying the abolitionist John Brown, students were shown the photograph of him taking a sacred pledge to destroy slavery. His right hand is raised as if he's being sworn in while his left hand holds the corner of a militant anti-slavery banner. In class, this same scene was then staged and each student photographed as they take took a "sacred" pledge of their choice, which they were spared from disclosing for a period of twenty years. This was a simulation, though maybe something more: an attempt to close the emotional distance between students and John Brown so they might feel the solemnity of a sacred pledge, the weight and moral burden of it. This entire activity took maybe twenty minutes.

Another piece of theater, which requires slightly more preparation, can involve a confrontation between a Dow Chemical campus recruiter and anti–Vietnam War protesters. Though brief, this exercise can still prove a good investment of time that pays off richly with a thoughtful discussion about free speech rights—and their limits. This activity takes maybe half a period.

Other simulations are more elaborate. This was the case in a course called Great Trials in American History, created for sophomores who had had a tough 9th-grade year and still needed to earn U.S. history credit. Although the students all shared the disappointment of past academic failure—whether because of inadequate skills, emotional issues, family problems, or all of those—there was actually a wide range of academic ability in the class. The course curriculum offered a concise survey of U.S. history, with each unit highlighting a famous legal case for study and/or reenactment.

Great Trials was intended to provide an academic experience that was informative, fun, participatory, and might help rebuild shattered confidence. The course was all about getting students back on their academic feet. As the course journeyed through American history, the curriculum would turn off the main highway onto ramps leading to the Salem witchcraft trials, the Boston Massacre trial, the trial of John Brown or Joe Hill, the Scopes trial, the Lindbergh kidnapping case, the Scottsboro Boys case, the Rosenberg case, and the My Lai massacre trial. Depending on the time available, students would take part in full or partial reenactments of these courtroom dramas.

Once roles were assigned (judge, lawyers, defendants, witnesses), students began the necessary preparation and research. These were not students who craved research projects, but the circumscribed and concrete nature of the task, the possibilities for hamming it up, and the prospect of courtroom victory proved highly motivating, if not irresistible.

Participation in these kinds of trial simulations deepens a student's understanding of the cases and also conveys the broader historical context at the same time. While role-playing strikes a good balance between fun and learning, students tend to take the work seriously. (Unlike other forms of group work, simulations require each person to play his or her role, and the kids quickly come to understand that.)

Trial simulations also generate considerable discussion. Should the accused witches confess? How could British soldiers be best defended? Might John Brown have been better served by an insanity defense? How best to impugn the testimony against the Scottsboro Boys? Were the Rosenbergs guilty, and if so, of what? What would have constituted fair punishment? Did William Calley commit war crimes in the village of My Lai?

During trial simulations, students had varied opportunities to excel, and the "outcomes" were often eye-opening. Many students who had given up on themselves, perhaps because they hated to write, turned out to have wonderful skills as litigators and orators. Teachers will no doubt observe quick minds at work, kids who can think on their feet, ask sharp questions, trip up witnesses, and sway juries to their side.

Best of all, one kind of success can and often will lead to another, even including the more conventional benchmarks—grades and test scores—that schools prize. Confidence and success are natural companions. Stars given a chance to shine often keep shining.

In 1990, as a result of declining enrollment, the Lincoln-Sudbury History Department requested permission and applied for grants to convert an empty classroom into a moot courtroom. Now, finally, the Great Trials class had a set worthy of its talents; its juridical cup truly did runneth over. Though the courtroom was eventually lost when the building was demolished, the students spent many intense courtroom hours in this beautiful facility, and quite a few of the legal tussles that took place in it were videotaped for posterity. But even a regular classroom can serve as a pretty fair moot courtroom once a few desks are rearranged. The power of imagination transcends all.

In another course, Postwar America, students took part in a different kind of three-day simulation. As part of a unit on the 1950s, several weeks were spent studying the domestic cold war, aka McCarthyism. By the time it came to the simulation, the students—more academically advanced than those in Great Trials—had done considerable reading and had viewed several documentaries about key events, including the House Un-American Activities Committee (HUAC) hearings.

When the appointed day arrived, students were nonchalantly asked if they would like to do something a little different for the next few days, namely, partake in a simulation of the HUAC. They were wildly enthusiastic about the prospect. Something different? Sure. Could be fun.

They were then informed that this was going to be a very realistic simulation, one that would only work if they promised to accept any punishment handed down by "the committee." "What kind of punishment?" they asked warily. "Oh, you might have to spend some of your free blocks in the classroom," they were told. However, they were also reassured that they would always be able to control their fate. If they didn't want detention, they could choose a strategy that would preserve their free time.

Caught between the unknown that intrigued them and the punishment they feared, students chose the simulation. Besides, they figured that they were smart enough to take on the HUAC. After all, hadn't they aced their SATs? The remainder of that class period was spent reviewing the menu of HUAC witness strategies and the several ways that the HUAC attempted to extract information from unwilling witnesses. The students asked when they were going to get their "identities" so they could figure out how to role-play most effectively. They were assured that their instructions would be distributed when the hearing was called to order next period. However, they were not told the truth, the whole truth, and nothing but the truth.

The chairman—aka the teacher—appeared at the hearing wearing a jacket and tie, so right away the students knew something was up. This Congressman Somebody-or-Other wielded a heavy gavel and a bad southern accent. He announced he would need some student colleagues to serve on the committee, to help keep records, and to make certain decisions and rulings. Twenty-five hands shot up into the air belonging to students who wanted to become volunteer congressmen. The chairman's tone was serious, student anxiety was rising, and becoming a committeeperson suddenly seemed the safest and most attractive option.

The chairman appeared to be selecting fellow committee members at random, but actually that decision had been made by the teacher the night before, with those students chosen who seemed the most vulnerable, who may not have had as many friends in class, and who therefore might find interrogation more uncomfortable.

The chairman asked his congressional "colleagues" to step into the hall, where they were told how the simulation would work. There would be no assigned roles and no information to hand out. Instead, students would play themselves. Moreover, questions would not be asked about their ties to international communism, after all, everyone could and would honestly testify that they had none. Rather, students would be asked, "Are you now or have you ever been a cheater?" and "Do you know anyone who has cheated?"

The committee then returned to the hearing room. Students were reminded of their vow to accept punishment, and the simulation was explained. They gasped. What does this have to do with the Cold War? they asked. The following explanation was provided: "The HUAC knows there is a Communist Party cell at the school that has encouraged cheating as a way to weaken the moral foundations of American society." This was stated as simple fact. The students didn't quite know what was going to happen, but they sensed they had fallen into a trap, which they had. (Later, the students would astutely point out that cheating was not a parallel issue to Communist Party affiliation, but they also came to realize that the issue at the heart of the simulation lay elsewhere.)

One after another, the students were called before the committee and sworn in. After an innocuous beginning, the committee members would pop the Big Question. At first, those who lied were treated gently, thus emboldening those who followed. But the hammer began to fall harder and penalties began to fly. Students started to tell unbelievable tales or even tried to smear members of the committee with accusations. Of course, this only made the chairman more indignant.

The committee huddled periodically to consider testimony. Perjury charges began to rain down, while grants of immunity were distributed strategically. The number of free-time detentions escalated: 5 . . . 10 . . . 15 . . . 20. Some students cooperated from the get-go. Some admitted to cheating and gave names to avoid the penalties given for past transgressions.

Others simply broke. In one class, an ex-boyfriend and girlfriend accused each other with genuine vehemence. Treachery only encouraged more of the same, and students began to turn on each other. By the end of the hearing, all those with detentions were given a last chance to cooperate with the committee. Most took it, and then the names really began to flow, names of other students in the class or of those in the other Postwar sections or those in other courses all together. Betrayal was in the air. Expediency ruled. People were getting dragged into the hearing testimony from every corner of the school.

For every name given, a certain number of detentions were erased. By now, committee members could hardly keep up with the number of alleged cheaters whose names were being offered. The dam of silence had been broken. Typically, only two or three members of the class were able to remain steadfast in their principled refusal to rat others out.

In pre-simulation essays, most students had written that they would never implicate friends or bend their knee to the HUAC. In post-simulation papers, students wrote of how hard it was to maintain their principles under pressure. Why didn't they? Well . . . they didn't want the detentions . . . and they got nervous . . . and they had so little free time as it was . . . and everyone else was doing it . . . and besides this was a game . . . but many felt ashamed and wished they could do it again.

They had planned to be courageous, and yet they crumbled. Welcome to history.

The simulation took three days. It would have taken considerably less time to simply hand out a story about one person's struggle with the HUAC. But would students have learned as much? Would the lesson have been as profound?

It's one thing to reflect on the moral conflicts engendered by appearing before the HUAC, and it's another to confront them. The simulation shed no light on communism during the 1950s, but it did illuminate how hard it is to remain true to oneself. It was a sobering lesson and not soon forgotten. If these students ever see again the acronym *HUAC*, even after high school becomes a distant memory, they may well think back to a certain hearing room and to the day the "Cold War came home" to their high school. (In fact, it had come home once before. Until the late 1960s, all Massachusetts teachers were required to sign a state loyalty oath as a condition of employment.)

The lasting impact of this exercise was confirmed when in February 2018, just after the school massacre in Parkland, Florida, a former student posted on Facebook about how important it was to speak out about things one considers wrong. She made the point while commenting about a classroom simulation that someone described in a recent post:

> My high school history teacher did something like this—with students fully informed that it was an experiment, but with the expectation that we'd serve any "detentions" we were given in the process—as part of our McCarthyism section. I totally failed, but learned from it that I shouldn't fall for that sort of fear-mongering again.

Here she was remembering back to an exercise that had taken place almost two decades before.

Postscript: Not long after state standardized testing began in Massachusetts in the 1990s, a Newton elementary school teacher wrote to the *Boston Globe* about how she would have to scrap an elaborate Constitutional Convention simulation that had become a well-loved tradition in her class. There was no time. What a shame.

Chapter Four

Field Trips On My Mind

Taking It On the Road

We are all schoolmasters, and our schoolhouse is the universe. To attend chiefly to the desk or schoolhouse while we neglect the scenery in which it is placed is absurd. If we do not look out we shall find our fine schoolhouse standing in a cow-yard at last.

—Henry D. Thoreau, *Journal*, October 15, 1859

Field trips are delightfully paradoxical. They take students out of school and out of their seats so they can learn more than they might have in school while fulfilling their state "seat time" requirement. These excursions are like "rebels *with* a cause," undermining routines and disrupting schedules, while promising at least a few periods' worth of relative freedom, adventure, and new vistas to take in.

In Twentieth Century American History classes, October meant a visit to the Newport mansions, those famed Rhode Island summer "bungalows" of America's first industrial barons. The trip was planned for early fall so the kids would have an early opportunity to interact with each other outside the classroom. That trip also helped put the student-teacher relationship on a friendlier footing and paid interpersonal dividends throughout the year, even if it meant visiting Newport a mind-numbing twenty times. If for no other reason, field trips, near and far, are invaluable in creating a class esprit.

THE NATION'S CAPITAL

For many years, Lincoln-Sudbury's sophomore class traveled to Washington, DC, for a long weekend to visit government buildings, memorials, and museums. This trip's rationale is self-evident. While we generally moved in class groups, our tenth graders were also given a degree of freedom. Organized in mini-groups of four or five, students were given an opportunity to use the metro and explore the city. Many students would later speak of the DC trip as a highlight of their high school years and a milestone in their growing up. The sites they visited in Washington—from the Lincoln and Vietnam memorials to the Holocaust Museum—made lasting impressions.

Of course, there is an elephant in this trip-planning room: money. Costs can vary widely. A day-long trip to Newport, Rhode Island, or even to New York City from Sudbury, Massachusetts, involves a relatively modest expense. But a trip to DC can cost hundreds of dollars for hotel rooms and transportation.

Many students and schools do not have the money for field trips. What to do? Most importantly, do not give up. At Lincoln-Sudbury, the school never assumed responsibility for financing trips, but most students came from families that could afford the expense. Typically, those who needed assistance were subsidized by what the great majority of the students were required to pay. If additional monies were needed, the students would organize bake sales or apply for grants from local foundations.

Today a new fundraising strategy has emerged: crowd-sourcing sites like GoFundMe. In fact, just recently, a Lincoln-Sudbury trip to Africa used this strategy on the Lincoln-Sudbury alumni Facebook page. The week-long civil rights tour of the Deep South described below was inspired by a trip first run by an urban public school, the Boston Arts Academy. Some years earlier, it had received grants from the Bill of Rights Project of the local ACLU chapter. Where there is a will, there is often a way.

If only money were the sole obstacle to organizing school trips! It's unfortunate that field trips, to say nothing of grade school recess and lunch periods, have taken heavy hits from accountability reforms. Many teachers now feel more pressure to "get through the material" and adhere to mandated frameworks. Is it possible to have a grimmer vision of education?

No one would argue that historical content is unimportant—how could any history teacher possibly do *that*? But field trip adventures can motivate students and spark their curiosity and imagination. The power of actual experience gained by traveling in a wider world is formidable. Today, where trips are concerned, teachers need to find the cracks in the wall and squeeze through them. There is no alternative to trying.

In this context, consider Thoreau's words: "What does education often do? It makes a straight-cut ditch of a free, meandering brook." In his journal, he recalls the influence of extracurricular lessons during his own grade school years.

> Berries are just beginning to ripen, and children are planning expeditions after them. They are important as introducing children to the fields and woods, and as wild fruits of which much account is made. During the berry season the schools have a vacation, and many little fingers are busy picking these small fruits. It is ever a pastime, not a drudgery. I remember how glad I was when I was kept from school a half a day to pick huckleberries on a neighboring hill all by myself to make a pudding for the family dinner. Ah, they got nothing but the pudding, but I got invaluable experience beside! A half a day of liberty like that was like the promise of life eternal. It was emancipation in New England. O, what a day was there, my countrymen! (*Journal*, July 16, 1851)

After Thoreau and his older brother John became teachers at the Concord Academy, they were enthusiastic organizers of field trips. Upon Thoreau's death, several of his former students wrote down their memories of these outings. Educator Martin Bickman provides more detail.

> There were frequent field trips, and not just to fields for nature study. The students were taken to the offices of a local paper to watch typesetting and to a gunsmith to watch the regulating of gunsights. In the spring, each student had a small plot of ploughed land to plant. In the fall of 1840 Henry brought in surveying instruments to teach his students yet another kind of field work in organizing a survey of Fairhaven Hill . . . This account of a river trip was reported by F. B. Sanborn (1884), one of Thoreau's early biographers, who himself later ran a progressive school in Concord: Henry Thoreau called attention to a spot on the river-shore, where he fancied the Indians had made their fires, and perhaps had a fishing village. . . . "Do you see," said Henry, "anything here that would be likely to attract Indians to this spot?" (Martin Bickman, *Minding American Education* [New York: Teachers College Press, 2003])

Once students had a chance to offer their own theories, Thoreau reportedly stuck his spade into the ground and—lo and behold!—uncovered an ancient Indian fire pit. What a wonderful example of pedagogy: first an experience . . . then an observation . . . then a question . . . then discussion . . . then "research" into the thesis.

During the 1970s, Lincoln-Sudbury, located only five miles from Walden Pond, was still basking in the glow of the innovative reform ideas of the 1960s. Rather than standardized testing, the watchword back then was unstandardized "experiential learning." This notion inspired an all-season, outward bound–type program called Nimbus that took students and teachers out into the woods for a *week* at a time. On some trips, students even embarked on "survival solos."

Of course, it is impossible to quantify what students gained from these experiences. How does one reduce to a data point a growth in self-confidence? Or learning how to work with a group? Or meeting the rigorous challenges of winter camping? How can one even begin to measure the cumulative impact of such experiences on the academic growth of students?

Here's a fact that may surprise some contemporary education reformers. The students who participated in Nimbus not only prized their memories but went on to become successful professionals, businessmen, teachers, artists, and tradespeople. How could this happen given all the "seat time" lost? Yet it happened.

There were also kids who hated school, saw no point to it, but stayed in school *only* because of programs like Nimbus and hands-on technology courses. They found meaning in the relationships forged with teachers while shivering in snow-covered tents in the White Mountains or sweating over a lathe in the wood shop. Among the faculty, there was a collective realization that what started a kid's engine was less important than the fact that it got started. Once their motors begin to hum, students can and do move out in different directions and with increasing speed. Readers, please give yourself this pop quiz: What experiences do you best remember from your high school years—and why?

Despite the increasing anxiety concerning college admissions, SAT scores, and transcripts even at progressive public schools like Lincoln-Sudbury, many teachers tried to keep experiential learning alive by continuing to organize trips. Not everyone was happy. An earnest young math colleague once cautioned that a student's future prospects might well be ruined by going on a one-day trip. She explained that his absence that day would make it nearly impossible for him to ever catch up. The teacher was assured that all would be well. Indeed, the student did survive and went on to a successful medical career.

There were two Lincoln-Sudbury history trips in particular that deserve a more detailed description.

NEW YORK CITY, HERE WE COME

In their Postwar America course, students were required to write analytical book discussions about J. D. Salinger's *Catcher in the Rye* and Jack Kerouac's *On the Road* as part of a background unit on the 1950s. A number of the backdrops that Salinger uses in his novel would be familiar to any native New Yorker. (Thank goodness, most New York City school kids are still taken to view the amazing dioramas at the American Museum of Natural History.)

And so was born a day-long New York trip, "In Search of Holden Caulfield and Jack Kerouac," that became a course tradition. Leaving Sudbury in early-morning darkness, we'd usually return close to 11 p.m.—a marathon trip always scheduled for a Friday or the day before a holiday.

At least in our imaginations, we would find Kerouac in a booth at the West End Bar & Grill on Broadway, at the Hungarian Pastry Shop, on the Columbia campus, or in the streets and coffee shops of Greenwich Village. We would catch up with Caulfield in the Natural History Museum, at Central Park's Pond, at the carousel (where we would take a ride in honor of Phoebe), and at rush hour inside the great vaulted space of Grand Central Station.

At each of these places, students took turns reading aloud the relevant passages from the novels. A few side trips were also included—after all, we were already in the city! A bus took us through Allen Ginsberg's "negro streets at dawn" to the Apollo Theater (a birthplace of rock and roll), to the eye-popping St. John the Divine Cathedral, to Tom's Restaurant (of Seinfeld fame) and to John Lennon's Strawberry Fields memorial. Years later, we would also visit Ground Zero.

Then there were the unexpected things that one can almost count on happening during a day in New York City. We bumped into movie stars. We got lost and wandered. We were approached by a panhandling homeless person who insisted, before accepting any money, that he first present an erudite analysis of the new gargoyles adorning the front of St. John the Divine. We posed with policemen and were invited to join a bridal picture with a beautiful Japanese couple being formally photographed at the Central Park Lake. We sang Beatles songs with wandering minstrels at the Imagine mosaic in Strawberry Fields. And naturally, at the carousel, we all tried to grab the brass ring.

Once the truly incredible occurred when serendipity slipped into over-drive. At the gates of Columbia University, where Kerouac attended school and met Allen Ginsberg, students were given an overview of the Beat move-ment. (The New York wandering trip had to be scheduled before winter set in, which was a few weeks before the class's formal study of the topic began.) They were then set loose to explore the Columbia campus while their teacher rushed off this particular year to meet a former student.

Because the bus had broken down in Connecticut, we had entered the city late and consequently our schedule was more hurried than usual. A young man with a camera, who was decidedly not in a hurry, approached. He had overheard the brief Beat overview and requested an interview. He seemed just one of the thousands of film students in New York. He was persistent, would not be put off, and was only allayed after being told when he should head to the group's designated gathering point by the famous Alma Mater statue.

One-half hour later, as the class reassembled, the group was approached by three very serious cameras. The film crew explained that they were mak-ing a documentary about Kerouac in New York and they wanted an encore of the introductory rap given at the Columbia gates. They also invited students to ask questions on camera. Eventually, those who spoke received checks drawn on the account of Beat Productions, practically sealing our member-ship in the Screen Actors Guild.

What really struck us was how Zen-like all of this was. We had to break down in Connecticut in order to arrive right on time in New York. Years later, when the students (now alumni) had long given up hope, the film was finally released as *The Source*—and they were in it. It earned high praise at the Sundance Film Festival and is still probably the best movie available on the Beats. It even had a good run in commercial theaters and was later shown on PBS as part of its *American Masters* series. The entire class had its fifteen minutes of fame.

The Caulfield/Kerouac field trip was nothing less than a mad dash around a city that some students, incredibly, had never visited. Arriving home, also in darkness, many in the class commented that they felt as though they had been gone for a week. What was accomplished? Surely not a single student's test scores rose as a result of this frenetic, nonstop rushing-about. But stu-dents loved the trip and remembered it fondly.

Yes, it definitely *was* fun and certainly beat a day in school. Nothing wrong with that. Sometimes fun can be its own excuse for being. Didn't Thoreau enjoy picking those huckleberries? But it also seemed that the students got much more out of the experience.

The Postwar America New York trip was a way to model for students how a passion for books can send a teacher on a four-hour, two-hundred-mile journey just to ride on the Central Park carousel and read Holden's concluding monologue about kids. They had a chance to soak up the great drama of New York's streets and to see and "feel" the landscapes that helped inspire the two novels.

This shared road-adventure might also help them to understand *On the Road* in a deeper way. Did they hear history whispering in the seedy booths at the West End Grill where Kerouac hatched "bop prosody" conspiracies with Ginsberg and, sadly, drank too much? Perhaps the trip also brought some spontaneity and adventure into their anxious, pressurized, and over-scheduled lives. Maybe they too would, in the words of Beat poet Lawrence Ferlinghetti, experience a "rebirth of wonder." That at least four couples fell in love on these trips and later married suggests that some of them did.

The trips to New York City continued despite a feeling shared by a few colleagues that nothing of consequence could be learned outside a school building. This collective search for Kerouac and Caulfield had a good shot at passing the "thirty-year test": that three decades later, students would be more likely to remember this trip (perchance with a smile) than most class meetings in math (or—ouch—in history).

"BEEN DOWN INTO THE SOUTH"

Taking students on a classroom with wheels that would roll to whatever place or topic we were studying remained a great dream. In 1993, Hofstra professor Douglas Brinkley got to this fantasy first. He loaded his students on a bus and spent an entire semester traveling hither and yon while discussing great authors. He even wrote a book about the experience, *The Majic Bus*. Thankfully, visions can't be copyrighted, and his success encouraged this teacher to keep dreaming.

The fantasy finally got its wheels and started rolling in 2001 when three colleagues helped to organize a trip following the Deep South trail of the civil rights movement, a major unit in the Postwar America course. Because of the distances involved, nothing less than a school vacation week would suffice, and as many students are involved in spring athletics, the trip opportunity was opened up to all juniors and seniors.

This arrangement also created the possibility of a more integrated experience. About 10 percent of the Lincoln-Sudbury student body is African American, most of them Boston residents who participate in METCO, a voluntary Massachusetts busing program. These students rarely had the chance to participate in the expensive school vacation trips to Europe and Latin America, which might cost as much as $2,000 or $3,000. Not only would a trip to the South be more affordable for them, it would give them an opportunity to explore firsthand this important chapter in their own history—and the nation's.

And so the April Vacation "Deep South" Trip was launched in 2001 and instantly became one of the school's most integrated student experiences. These trips—four in all—unleashed the full power of history in ways that the chaperons had not planned or even been prepared for.

Not that there wasn't planning. There was plenty of that. In fact, it took more than 100 emails to the charter bus company, the airlines, prospective speakers, museums, and motels as well as emails to keep parents and the trip participants in the loop. All told, planning, collecting money, doing publicity, raising scholarship funds (the trip cost about $800 for travel and motel accommodations) almost became an extra part-time job for the organizers.

But was it ever worth it! We were determined to avoid a charter company–like trip with bus drivers reading packaged scripts. We wanted the experience to be as close to the bone, as raw and honest, as it could be.

The itinerary of the trip was simple enough: fly to Memphis to meet the bus, drive south through Mississippi to Louisiana and New Orleans, and then turn east to Birmingham and finally Atlanta seven days later.

Along the way, the students visited civil rights museums, memorials, and the sites of major demonstrations, but only after first viewing brief documentary clips on the bus VCR about what had occurred in these very places four decades earlier.

We managed to get off the beaten track as well, visiting the small town of Philadelphia, Mississippi, where three civil rights workers were murdered in 1964, and later the gravesite of one of them, James Chaney. It had been placed deep in the countryside in an unsuccessful attempt to protect it from Ku Klux Klan desecration.

Destinations of cultural significance—such as the Delta Blues Museum and Mound Bayou, Mississippi, one of the last black-owned and -governed townships in the United States—were a highpoint. And there was also time for fun at Graceland—the home of a singer who became very successful covering black music—and later listening to jazz on the streets of New Orleans' French Quarter.

In retrospect, the trip proceeded in multiple dimensions simultaneously. One journey took the group over the landscape of a region that few young people from the Northeast ever see. Here we encountered music, food, vegetation, views, and accents with which we were not familiar. Outside the bus windows: shotgun shanties, cotton fields, crawfish, gumbo, grits, juke joints, blues, jazz, zydeco, kudzu vines, heat. This was an American Studies course on wheels that opened eyes and ears, fed us, and made us sweat.

Another simultaneous journey led us through time zones, literally and historically. In 2002, students rode through Mississippi just as voters were deciding whether to keep their Confederacy-inspired state flag (which they did, to great collective distress among the students). On two later trips, we arrived in cities and towns to find preparations under way to finally try men accused of the bombing and shooting of civil rights activists decades before. The South was coming to terms with its own history, and the scales of justice were finally being balanced—at least a bit. Yes indeed, "the past is never dead." We were driving through the history of the South, with ghosts, echoes, shadows moving all around us.

There was also an emotional dimension of the trip that took us more deeply into ourselves. This was unexpected on the first trip and still a surprise on the subsequent ones. At various points, we stopped to talk with community leaders and movement veterans. One had walked with Dr. King from Selma to Montgomery. Another was a crusading white journalist, committed to his native region and still determined to see justice done in the case of the Philadelphia, Mississippi, murders. There was the unofficial historian of Mound Bayou who had dedicated his life to preserving the history of a unique town built by free blacks.

And finally, there was an original member of the Freedom Singers who had shared songs of freedom at so many civil rights rallies in the 1960s. He told his life story, from Jim Crow victim to freedom fighter to community organizer, and he got the group singing the great songs of the movement. We heard our own voices. Cynicism evaporated. Tears flowed. The freedom spirit he spoke of became palpable and carried students beyond facts to something alive and inspiring that no textbook can possibly evoke.

Finally, there was a dimension of the journey that can simply be called THE BUS, into which thirty-six students and four teachers were crammed for many hours each day. Here was a journey of a kind as well: chances taken, tentative at first, and bridges thrown across scary chasms. Students who once walked past each other in the hallways of their school became friends. The suburbs met the city. Black and white together. They laughed. They sang freedom songs, Dylan songs, Southern songs, goofy songs, and hip-hop. They slept on the shoulders of those who had been strangers a week before.

What a contrast to the self-segregation of kids in so many American high schools. When students are given a meaningful context in which to relate, they find each other. Fragile tendrils of trust had time to grow.

The Deep South trips gave students the opportunity to see their country and to encounter past and present in an intense way. For some, the trips were life-altering. Right after the 2001 trip, students shared their reflections. One wrote,

> My trip down South was a wake-up call. I came back feeling a deep connection to God, to my peers, to history, and to the world around me. I have come back with this amazing determination to walk in the footsteps of those who have made momentous changes. It can be done, we do have the power to make history. But I have also realized it will require a lot of work to sustain the feeling of empowerment. I cannot give in to the sudden feeling of helplessness. I know this is just the beginning of my personal journey of discovery . . . I can proudly say my heart is more committed now than it has ever been.

And another had this to say:

> I came to one major conclusion about the whole thing: it opened my eyes. I went down to the South with a vision of a place that simply did not exist, and in seven days, had that picture totally obliterated and a whole new one erected in its place. I met people who were like no one I had ever imagined, saw places I hadn't ever dreamed were real, and realized what it was like to be in a place where history was made. I had never appreciated Boston before in the way I did when I first journeyed downtown after I got home from the South. I thought of the quotation that hung in my classroom all year, "Unless you feel a thing, you can never guess its meaning." Suddenly it made a lot of sense. We went down South to understand it on a level no book or movie ever would have given us. To understand the South, and the Civil Rights Movement, and what it all really meant, we simply had to be there.

In 2005, just a few weeks after we had left Philadelphia, Mississippi, and returned home, a man was finally convicted for his role in the murders of three civil rights workers forty years before. We had followed the case closely, and the day before the verdict came down, a Boston student sent this email to her fellow trip participants:

> Court TV is following the case from beginning to end so try to catch some of it. As I told the teachers, this is all very exciting because we know so much about this case, and we all now share a part of history.

When the verdict finally came down, she wrote again: "We won! Justice! I am really excited!"

In *Leaves of Grass*, Walt Whitman tells us that the "universe has many roads . . . roads for traveling souls." Teachers, you just might want to get your Google Maps out.

Chapter Five

History Begins At Home

Is It Knocking On Your Door?

History is not just something that happened long ago and far away. History happens to all of us all the time. Local history brings history home, it touches your life, the life of your family, your neighborhood, your community.

—Thomas J. Noel, historian

Local history is like a subtle earth tremor. We are barely conscious of the history in front or behind us, to say nothing of what's under us. It's all over the place—maybe too close—and so is rendered nearly invisible. Once perceived, it becomes unforgettable, both the indelible landmarks and the consciousness of how the "mystic chords of memory" tie past to present. All the richness of the past-—the drama, the hardships, the struggles, the triumphs—surround our school buildings. The stage is everywhere, and the actors lived in our own cities and towns.

VISITING ANOTHER SCHOOL

In April 2014, the University of Massachusetts, Boston education program required that a formal observation be made of one of its most talented practicum students. The young man had been assigned to Walpole High School, and on that day he was teaching a lesson about the Vietnam War. His students seemed quite engaged, and one asked if Walpole had been affected by the conflict. The student-teacher responded that he wasn't sure, but that he didn't think so.

A good, honest answer. But a better answer could be found in the lobby area by the school's main entrance that visitors must walk through to get to the history wing. There on a wall, prominently displayed, was a large plaque in memory of a Walpole High alumnus who had been killed in Vietnam. Like much of local history, the Vietnam War–Walpole connection was hiding in plain sight.

That same year history intruded again on Walpole High School, and the story even found its way into the mass media. The school's sports teams have long been known as the Rebels, and when Walpole athletes took the field, cheerleaders led the way with a Confederate flag. With the 150th anniversary of the end of the Civil War only a year away, there was some statewide controversy about this choice of mascot and symbol.

Most of the pressure to make a change seemed to come from outside the town. To make matters even more complicated, after the school had decided to ditch the flag, an alumnus whose home abutted the football field erected on his property line a tall flagpole with a giant Confederate flag.

Tradition was sacred to many at Walpole High, and there was considerable resistance to making any further change. In the course of this controversy, neither the media nor townspeople made note of the fact that twelve citizens of the town had died and over one hundred had fought to defeat that rebel flag and all it stood for. O history, history!

There is more cause for humility than self-righteousness in relating this story. No one knew less about the history of the towns he had worked in than a certain Lincoln-Sudbury educator who would later become a practicum supervisor.

What follows is the unlikely story of that teacher's growing awareness of the tremors shaking the ground beneath him and how this realization enriched his career. The discoveries made are available to all who can find the time to look around. Actually, that's the hard part. Between preparing, teaching, grading, and writing college recommendations, it's not so easy for teachers—or anyone really—to find the time, but it is very much worth trying.

A BRONX BOY IN THE 'BURBS

No one who enters Sudbury, Massachusetts, can remain unaware for long that it's an old town. The even more venerable namesake towns of Lincoln and Sudbury can still be found in England, but the sign on this "newer" town's border informs you it was founded in 1639. That passes for ancient in the United States.

Driving to the high school from the old town center takes a visitor right by the old revolutionary war burial ground where many of those interred died a century before our independence struggle began. Henry Ford's reconstruction of the burned out Wayside Inn (of Longfellow poem fame) is now a dining place reserved for memorable family occasions. Just up the road from the inn stands a reconstructed "old" grist mill.

The people who live in the town certainly take pride in Sudbury's lineage—colonial-style mini-mansions abound—but much of that distant past has been obliterated by the suburban development that began just after World War II. Sudbury is now an affluent bedroom community for busy parents who work in Boston.

When he commenced commuting out to the school in 1973, this teacher almost expected to be stopped by passport control. Growing up in the Bronx meant that suburbs—and this town—were a mystery, a place in some parallel universe. Later, a strong connection would be forged to the school but not to the town it was placed in. In the U.S. Survey course, a brief reference was made to Sudbury's role in the famous North Bridge battle in neighboring Concord where the "shot was fired heard 'round the world." In Postwar America, Sudbury got an encore cameo appearance as an example of a post–World War II middle-class suburb.

How surprising then to learn many years later that this Bronx boy actually had a personal, if indirect, connection to the town through his mother-in-law, whose maiden name was Puffer. Her ancestors had been early settlers in the town, and one even became a captain of the Sudbury militia during the Revolution. (In the early nineteenth century, this branch of the Puffers would migrate to western Massachusetts.)

One morning, a historical marker, passed a thousand times before on the route home, caught this commuter's eye and signaled him to pull over. The marker noted that on that very spot the townsfolk of Sudbury had repulsed an Indian attack in a battle that proved to be a turning point in the King Philip's War of 1676. A memorial stone on the site reminded visitors that as result of the battle, the town had been "saved." (Some historians go even further in suggesting that the victory saved the entire Massachusetts Bay Colony.)

The simple memorial inscription suggested this outcome was unquestionably a good thing, a bias that speaks volumes about the challenge of studying history. Where had this marker been hiding during the previous thirty years' worth of commuting mornings? Apparently, a certain teacher had just sped by, probably preoccupied by that day's lesson plans about Native Americans and colonial history.

MEETING MR. THOREAU

What really gave this by now familiar commuting landscape a new aspect were kayaking trips later taken on the Sudbury River under bridges motorists crossed every morning and afternoon, often with only a vague awareness of the water flowing beneath. Kayaking on this quiet river introduced a world of nature unfamiliar to this native New Yorker.

That discovery soon led to another . . . to Henry David Thoreau, the great transcendentalist writer whose spirit hovers over the area. He loved these local rivers, which he described as "the only unfenced nature hereabouts." If memory serves, Thoreau received a brief mention in the New York State Regents curriculum that all Bronx kids had to contend with. Thoreau built a cabin. He had refused to pay his taxes as a protest against slavery and the Mexican War. He had spent a night in jail. Was there really anything more to know?

It turned out there was a good deal more, and finding it involved a passionate immersion in local history. How surprising to later learn that Thoreau frequently sauntered through Sudbury, walking right by the present location of Lincoln-Sudbury Regional High School. In fact, according to his journal, it was at Nobscot Hill in Sudbury that he wondered if future generations of Americans would ever know the taste of a wild apple. And yes, in his epic two-million word, more than seven-thousand-page journal, Thoreau describes his occasional encounters with the Puffer family, especially "Pigeon-Catcher" Puffer.

Out of this unexpected Thoreau "meet-up" grew a course called Meet Mr. Thoreau, which encouraged some new pedagogical initiatives, including organizing the construction of a replica of Thoreau's cabin, a project that is described in chapter 7.

The Thoreau elective—which met only twice a week—provided the opportunity to explore this one aspect of local history in depth. Much of this Thoreau curriculum can be found at http://www.schechsplace.org/content/THOREAU/MEETMRTHOREAUCOURSE/0contents.html.

The core of the course was fairly traditional, though with an important difference. During the semester, students were responsible for reading four of

Thoreau's essays: *Walking*; *Civil Disobedience*; *A Plea for Captain John Brown*; and *Life Without Principle*. Discussions were led in seminar style by the students themselves, each of whom presented the pages assigned to them. Along with these readings, the course utilized the school's technology shop for hands-on projects like making pencils, albeit of a more fanciful design than those Thoreau and his father manufactured.

The class also spent considerable time outdoors to give students the opportunity to fully ponder Thoreau's thought that "it's not what you look at, it's what you see." Trees that only yesterday were passed by as strangers were now identified and named. Time was spent writing journal observations of natural phenomena and journeying back through history during a field trip to nearby Concord. In one day, the class visited Thoreau's birthplace, the public school he had worked in, the museum that displayed artifacts belonging to him, the spot where he was jailed, his last residence, and his final resting place on Authors' Ridge in Sleepy Hollow Cemetery.

The group was also welcomed into the Thoreau Institute and then into the Special Collection Room of the Concord Library, where Thoreau's original manuscripts and surveys are preserved. All these historical riches were close at hand and ripe for the picking.

How fortuitous that Walden Pond was located only five miles from our school! Even so, there had been no regular field trips to the pond from Lincoln-Sudbury before Meet Mr. Thoreau was created, and this was true even when freshmen were reading parts of *Walden* in their American Lit classes. (Imagine if earth science classes at Grand Canyon High School neglected to organize field trips to the canyon!) While our proximity to Walden was a unique gift, distance is not a fatal disadvantage when it comes to observing nature. As the Thoreau Institute likes to remind us, "Walden is everywhere."

One of the most memorable course field trips involved almost no movement on our part: watching the sun rise at Walden. With the special permission of the park rangers, the class was allowed to arrive at the pond around 5:00 a.m., before the park officially opened. The students proceeded to sit on the stone wall that borders the southern edge of the pond, watching the imperceptible transition from pitch black dark to golden light, from silence to bird song cacophony. No one spoke. Some wrote down notes for their own journals. Mostly students just stared across the black waters as the curtain was slowly raised in this theater called Nature.

When the sun was up, and golden mists began drifting across Walden, the group walked around the pond and back to the stone wall, at which point maybe a dozen brave souls took the chilly October plunge, much as Thoreau once did. And, yes, their cries rose to the heavens.

The goal of the course was to acquaint students with the thoughts and writings of Henry David Thoreau, but more than that, to expose students to some of what he experienced—without necessarily being explicit—so they could compare, consciously or unconsciously, their responses to his on the subjects of nature, civil disobedience, violence, and social values. Thoreau was therefore both the subject and a co-participant in all discussions. In this way, the course attempted to foster a continuing conversation across the century-and-one-half since his death.

Thoreau and nature clearly conspired to encourage my students to produce unusually creative writing. Thoreau set the example of taking writing seriously, and perhaps this is why students handed in assignments that seemed more authentic than most homework. If the subject matter inspired them, their work certainly inspired the teacher. And so, every year, with the help of student editors, their writings were bound in a volume filled with their exceptionally thoughtful and deeply felt reflections.

THE PERILS OF BUILDING STONE WALLS

Local history unexpectedly emerged one other time when the school celebrated its fortieth anniversary in 1995. To commemorate the occasion, a group of seniors decided they wanted to add a historical touch to our nondescript building and create a new tradition at the same time. The idea was to build a section of a classic New England stone wall in front of the school that each succeeding graduation class would add its own section to. We just needed the stones. Unexpectedly, this failed project ended up uncovering the hidden history of the school, which, as it turned out, was still an open wound for some.

But failure lay in the future when the "Stone Wall Taskforce" first went into action. Seniors mobilized. Local stone wall artisans volunteered to help. Plans were drawn up. Rocks of manageable size were soon found in the woods behind the school along an old tumble-down wall. (The fieldstone in the local stone yard was too expensive). The wall seemed practically built. One could already imagine students returning forty years hence, grey-haired and stooped, to show their grandkids "the section of wall we built in '95."

Practically built, but not quite. The head of the building and grounds department raised an interesting question. The tumble-down wall might serve as a property marker. How did the owners on the other side feel about our culling rocks from this wall? There were still a few days to go before Senior Week when the wall would have to be built, so a group of students was designated to go to the abutter to ask for their permission. The town clerk helpfully identified who the abutter was.

It turned out the land bordering the school had been placed in a trust controlled by Mrs. Carol Wolfe, the owner's daughter. Members of the task-force went to her house, where her husband, Mr. Wolfe, greeted them at the door. They explained the proposed "stone wall tradition" and made their request. Some felt almost silly asking for permission to take some rocks, but they understood the need to make a formal request.

Mr. Wolfe, like his wife, was a graduate of the very first graduating class of Lincoln-Sudbury. He listened politely but then quietly began to shake his head. He responded in a way that suggested this was a weightier matter than the students could ever know. The delegation began to get a sinking feeling. "No," he said, "I don't think she'll ever agree. She's never gotten over it." But who was "she"? And what was "it"?

"She" was Carrie Waite, Mr. Wolfe's mother-in-law, who was still very much alive and lived right down the road. She was ninety-two years old and probably wouldn't even agree to hear the seniors' request, he said. The students asked if they could speak to her directly because maybe they could better explain the spirit of the stone wall vision. "Nope, it'll just make it worse," Mr. Wolfe said. "She hates the high school." It seems that Mrs. Waite had been nursing a grudge for a very long time, but he promised to speak to her and leave a message at the school.

As the students were leaving, Mr. Wolfe pointed out another large tract of land owned by the family. "We can't even find anyone to farm it anymore," he told them. Still, he said, Mrs. Waite won't consider selling it off for development. She wants to keep the land open.

A written history of our school, completed some years before, correctly noted that Lincoln-Sudbury had been built on land purchased from a farm. But now we learned that the school had actually been built on the land of two farms. One farmer willingly sold his land, while the other had it seized by eminent domain. That latter farm had belonged to Carrie Waite's family going back to the seventeenth century. She had loved the farm and particular-ly the woodlots she wandered in as a child. These were taken to create the athletic fields at Lincoln-Sudbury. The students' project had inadvertently walked smack dab into a very painful chapter in the town's past.

A few days later, the school registrar retrieved a voice message that Mr. Wolfe had left on the school phone: "Hello, about that stone wall project, our family will unfortunately have to ask you not to take the stones."

So this ends up being the story of how an idea to build a stone wall ran into the stone wall of history and the long memory of a ninety-two-year-old woman who still wanted her woodlots back. Whether in Palestine or on own Concord Road, the past is not easily forgotten—or forgiven.

We had studied the suburbanization of Sudbury during the 1950s unit of Postwar America. Apparently, the building of the regional high school was a devastating defeat for the "townies" that were trying to stem the suburban tide and preserve the farming town they had grown up in. From 1740 to 1940, the population of Sudbury had only increased by 100 inhabitants.

In class, this period had seemed part of a dead past, a carcass for high school students to dissect, a few dates, and a landmark or two—that is, until the Stone Wall Project uncovered something still very raw. Mr. Wolfe later told us that Ms. Waite, who lived to become the town's oldest resident, sometimes sat in her rocking chair up there on the hill looking down at the high school and what was left of her beloved woodlots.

Local history comes free and is waiting out there to be rediscovered. So many stories surround us, and all of them are "locally sourced." If you search for them or just keep your ear to the ground, you may be surprised by what you find and very grateful that you made a vital connection between an academic curriculum and the world right outside your classroom windows.

INTERLUDE . . .

Morning Request
My students asked to shut
off the lights.
We want to show you something,
they said.
Through the window rushed
a haystack's worth
of autumn light,
and we just sat,
amazed,
and glowed.

October 1994

Chapter Six

Taking History Into the Hallways

Seed-Time of an Epiphany

Small things start us in new ways of thinking.

—V. S. Naipaul, *A Bend in the River*

The challenges of teaching morph but never quite disappear. New teachers have to struggle their way through even a brief forty-minute class while enduring the slow-motion torture of the classroom clock. Even experienced teachers have to work hard to keep their material fresh and energy levels high. For mid-level veterans, with ten or fifteen years in, the first telltale signs of burnout may become apparent. It doesn't help when teachers have no overall philosophy of teaching beyond "whatever works" and whatever promises to get them through the next day. This is written from personal experience.

There are two metaphors that come to mind. The first is daunting: A mountain stands between a teacher and the summer, and if you want to get there, to lie in some hayfield in Vermont watching a billowy cloud drift lazily across the sky, you have to climb that mountain to come down the other side. Along the way, there will be lesson plans to devise, materials to find, papers to grade, recommendations to write, trips to organize, kids to help—so many details to deal with that if you actually knew how many, you might not even bother attempting the climb in the first place.

The second metaphor is hopeful. Buoyed by the good days and taking on serious water on the bad are the normal vicissitudes of a teacher's working life. The job is absorbing, but is it really possible to sustain the energy required for another decade or even two? Fortunately, the school year bears a resemblance to the baseball season. You can lose some games and still have a very successful season. Much as for baseball players, this reality can keep a teacher going even after a discouraging losing streak.

Another often unexpected source of support for teachers, communicated through evaluations, is that students may think their teachers are doing a better job than they themselves do. If one cares enough, it is easy to become overly self-critical.

In the mid-1980s, the new Postwar America class happened to be loaded with friends and tons of *je ne sais quoi* . . . spirit! During an unrelentingly rainy week in March, a student suggested we do a class project. "Great idea," another student responded, "but like what?" From somewhere in the back of the room, a voice rang out, "Let's paint a mural." Hmm. This seemed doable because we just happened to have two very talented artists in the class.

A MURAL APPEARS

To make a year-long story short, students successfully designed and painted a "60s Mural" in the hallway near our classroom during their free time. This artwork became a well-loved feature of the school and helped make Lincoln-Sudbury's building visually unique. This was no generic "spirit" display that one can find in many schools. No, this was a passionate mural about history that colorfully captured the utopian hopes and struggles of the period. It expressed a point of view that emerged from student discussions about that turbulent time.

The two student artists made a plan, painted the faces, and blocked out work for others. The kids ended up working on it all year, even during school vacations. With tarps on the floor and some good rock playing on a boom box, they worked as if they had been transported to a planet without clocks. The mural wrapped around two walls, and when June arrived, it was almost but not quite finished. Alumni returned after their freshman year in college to complete it.

In the Lincoln-Sudbury of that time, no permission was required to paint a mural. Perhaps this was because no one had thought to paint one in the hallways before, and so the students just went out and did it. The superintendent did express mild concern when informed that the paint would cost about a hundred dollars. A conservative school committee member, whose son had worked on the mural, later said the money was the best the school had ever spent. The project had helped turn his kid—one of the lead artists—in a positive direction.

Later, the 60s Mural would be dedicated to the memory of three civil rights workers murdered in 1964, and we received beautiful letters from their parents. Hearing from them changed the nature of the project. What began as a suburban school art project became a vehicle connecting the class to the bloody history of the civil rights movement. And from that one mural, a school mural movement sprang up. Soon a mural was painted celebrating women's history and another commemorating a school walkout at the time of the Rodney King trial. These murals brought color and a sense of history into the everyday life of the school.

The old school building was demolished in 2004, and until its last day these murals were treated with reverence. Alumni even returned to be photographed in front of them. They were so beloved that two years before the demolition, graduation classes and local foundations provided the money to create full-scale reproductions that would hang in the new building, which one day would also be decorated with its own original mural art.

What wasn't apparent at the time was how profoundly the mural project would change this teacher's understanding of what teaching could mean. It was as if a mental door had swung open and an epiphany entered with two questions: "Why teach only in a classroom?" and "Why not see part of a teacher's role as bringing history into the larger life of the school?"

In other words, why couldn't history teachers do their best to historicize their school environment in the same way that advertising firms market their products by eroticizing our popular culture?

While some school-wide history and civics projects had attracted student and faculty attention, among them a long but ultimately successful effort to replace the school's Native American sports mascot, these were one-off, ad hoc efforts. (Three decades later, the Massachusetts Legislature debated whether to ban school Native American mascots state-wide.) But the mural project crystalized the idea of bringing history into the school's hallways on a regular basis.

Acting on this "hallway epiphany" became a major focus. Without the support and participation of colleagues, none of the initiatives described below could have succeeded. The goal of "hallway history" was to reinforce the importance of the subject, to deepen interest and empathy, and to encourage community discussions, some of which found their way back into the classroom.

ECHOES, THE HISTORY MAGAZINE

If the mural project inspired an effort to "do history" outside the classroom, another development gave this effort a greater sense of urgency. By the mid-1980s, computers had made their appearance in schools and naturally there was a great fascination with them. Enrollment in computer classes shot up in high schools and colleges. This development was accompanied by reports of declining enrollment in the humanities, a trend that has not only continued but accelerated.

The humanities needed defending even in our little corner of the academic world. A couple of us in the department thought a history magazine might be a good way to begin. It seemed unfortunate that while wonderful work was being done by students, no one ever saw it but the teachers. Why couldn't it be more widely shared so young historians would receive the validation of seeing their work in print? This might also help encourage others to reach for high standards of excellence. Further, by showcasing outstanding work the magazine could also help make clear what "outstanding" meant. For many striving students, that standard remained a mystery.

These ideas came together in the creation of *Echoes, the History Magazine*, published by Lincoln-Sudbury biannually between 1984 and 1994. At the time, *Echoes* was one of the few high school history magazines in the country, and there probably aren't too many today. We started out by reprinting exceptional history essays and papers recommended by teachers and evaluated by the magazine's student staff. Later, although classroom work would still be printed, the editors would decide on a theme for an issue and ask their staff to write related articles. Some of the featured themes were Humor and History, Women's History, Sex and History, National Politics, and Gay History.

Naturally, the staff had to struggle to get the funding to print the issues. The good news is that today the whole project could be done online for free.

One *Echoes* issue in particular stirred up considerable controversy. Gay history was not considered an appropriate topic in many high schools in the early 1990s. In wide swaths of the country, this is still true. The *Echoes* issue exploring the history of this subject caused a minor national sensation. The cover photo depicted a line of nine students staring at the reader, with a tenth student in the middle, back turned and only his Lincoln-Sudbury jacket visible. The banner headline on the cover read "One in Ten."

The appearance of a high school magazine on a gay theme led to an article in the *Boston Globe*, which was then picked up and carried far and wide by the Associated Press. We received a few angry notes from local parents, but the students also had the chance to read many touching letters from gay adults and students across the country. Many thanked the editors and recounted their terrifying years in high school. The issue showed that high school students could handle controversial topics with maturity, thoughtfulness, and courage.

Echoes published for only ten years but ended its run with a bang. Two years before ceasing publication, the magazine's last and very able staff decided to write a book about the history of the school. There was a sense of mission surrounding this project because earlier that same year the state had passed an education reform law mandating standardized testing. While this top-down change would take years to be implemented, the students feared for the future of Lincoln-Sudbury and wanted to preserve its history as a progressive and slightly eccentric school.

Two years and one hundred oral history interviews later, a paperback book: *". . . A Different Kind of Place": A History of Lincoln-Sudbury Regional High School, 1954–1994*, appeared in time for the school's fortieth anniversary. For the *Echoes* staff, this was a major learning experience. It's one thing to talk about studying history in a class. It's another to face, as all working historians do, the problems of research, periodization, interpretation, organization, and writing. They worked hard and met during school, after school, on school vacation weeks, and during summer break. The student editors rose to the occasion. But for them to rise, they had to be given the opportunity. How easy it would have been for their teachers to say, "Impossible. Forget it." Many thought we should have said just that, but how wrong we would have been.

ROLLING WITH HISTORY: THE MAGIC OF OLD AV CARTS

Most of the "history in the hallway" projects described here were collaboratively planned and implemented by students and teachers working together. Most arose from units being taught in our classes, world developments, or historical anniversaries. This was not the case with another initiative that students assisted with, but which did not arise from any course lessons. It was a surprise to all. No one saw it coming.

Every teacher finds a way to move materials from room to room. Mine involved the bad habit of carrying two heavy canvas bags loaded up with notebooks, grading papers, and handouts, swinging like pendulums. Cleaning them out occasionally would have helped, but who had the time? This went on for years. A member of the Building and Grounds crew pointed out that this could cause a shoulder injury, but the warning was blithely ignored until the inevitable morning arrived when the bags could no longer be lifted, let alone swung.

Next stop: physical therapy. Meanwhile, the Audiovisual Department was kind enough to provide an old cart that served as a rolling conveyance for the usual classroom cargo. The cart was old, dented, drab green, and badly in need of some sprucing up. After a few days, it was decorated with a sign on the front sporting the single word "Further," an homage to the name of Ken Kesey's Merry Pranksters hippie bus that students had just read about in Postwar. Soon after, a red blinking bicycle light was added to help navigate the crowded hallways.

After about a week, the thought arose: wouldn't it be better to push an actual rough facsimile of Ken Kesey's bus through the halls of the school, augmented with Bob Dylan singing from somewhere in the engine block? This would provide a nice visual and aural echo of the period under study. Student artists helped transform the cart into something that came straight out of Haight-Ashbury. When the cart turned a corner and encountered a crowd blocking the hallway, headlights would flash and the horn would beep. Students would look annoyed, until they turned around, took a look . . . and then their faces would register sheer delight. They were experiencing history as pure whimsy.

But if one cart was good, then wouldn't two be much better? Admittedly, this is a very American way of thinking. Ultimately, this second cart realized a dream of pushing an AV–cart replica of the Fitchburg Railroad cars that ran by Walden in Thoreau's time. A layout of the pond was created on top while a battery-powered model train circled round it, accompanied by recorded train sounds. Thus did "Walden a la Cart" roll from class to class with books and handouts safely tucked inside the contraption. Student artists are certainly capable of amazing things in the service of history.

Unexpectedly, the carts had a life beyond Lincoln-Sudbury, ending up in a Lowell, MA, museum exhibit featuring "rolling art." A curator actually considered the carts folk art worthy of display. But art or no, the carts showed that the humorous and eccentric also have a place in the serious business of education. In a literal way, they facilitated taking history into the hallways and even rolled history right through them. Amused colleagues pushing more conventional rolling stock usually gave the carts the right-of-way, perhaps because they appreciated seeing pedagogy on the move.

HISTORICAL COMMEMORATIONS

Part of historicizing the culture of the school involved acknowledging important holidays and anniversaries, as well as Lincoln-Sudbury's own history. Besides its regular issues, the *Echoes* staff also published a series of reprints on major historical holidays—Lincoln's birthday, Thanksgiving, Mother's Day, etc.—so that students would know a little more about what they were supposedly celebrating.

For example, on Lincoln's birthday, students would hand out a pamphlet with a few of his incomparable speeches. This modest compilation was an attempt to rescue our arguably greatest president from the new car ads that feature him on President's Day. What a fate for this soulful, resolute hero of millions!

The Lincoln commemoration was also joined to a display that took almost no time to assemble. Every February 12 the staff would place an oversize photograph of him in the window of the school's main office and would post underneath it a few lines from a poem about him. Often it was just these simple lines from Walt Whitman's *Leaves of Grass*:

This Dust Was Once the Man

This dust was once the man,
Gentle, plain, just and
under whose cautious hand,
Against the foulest crime in history known in any land or age,
Was saved the Union of these States.

or this even briefer one,

Abraham Lincoln (Born February 12, 1809)

To-day from each and all, a breath of prayer, a
Pulse of thought,
To memory of him—to birth of him

Yes, just the barest pulse of remembrance. Who knows how many students noticed this modest display as they rushed by the large plate-glass window, but if even a few did, the effort seemed worth it. The Lincoln birthday initiative also serves as a prime example of how one idea can lead to another. In the reprint, the editors had expressed a desire to "demonstrate the power of the spoken word." A few years later, this sentiment led to the launching of the History Oratory Competition, which became a popular event sponsored by the History Department for nearly two decades. This activity was just a part of the effort to unlatch the schoolhouse gate and welcome history in.

FROM COLUMBUS . . . TO MANDELA

Some commemorations were more elaborate others. On the 500th anniversary of Columbus's voyage, placards were placed around the school calling attention to the positive and negative aspects of the "Columbian Exchange." Throughout the week, students could follow the explorer's progress by scaled markings on the floor around the school, showing the dates when he and his crew reached different lines of longitude. As Columbus sailed across the ocean, he was also turning corners on the flat earth of Lincoln-Sudbury's hallways.

Years later, students would rise to celebrate the release of Nelson Mandela and to honor the enormous sacrifices he had made to end the South African Apartheid system. This commemoration was a study in simplicity. It took but a minute but was very powerful.

WORLD WAR II

There were other observances that were also very simple but hopefully had a cumulative impact. On the fiftieth anniversary of Pearl Harbor, our principal made a PA announcement asking students to rise in remembrance of the sailors who perished on that "day of infamy." The announcement was followed by the playing of the famous news bulletin that broke into the regularly scheduled radio programs on one long-ago December 7.

On the fiftieth anniversary of D-Day, students were startled by the PA system when it broadcast into every corner of the school the four musical notes from Beethoven's Fifth that signaled the beginning of the mighty invasion, followed by the principal reading Roosevelt's stirring public prayer for that day. For the half-century anniversary of the end of World War II, students were kept abreast of the final battles and shrinking distance to Berlin by giant blow-ups and banners in the main hallway and notations in the printed daily announcements ("100 miles to go!").

On the final, climactic day of victory, V-E Day plus fifty, the principal read Norman Corwin's great radio narrative, "Take a bow, GI! Take a bow little guy!" What a moving remembrance!

The Class of 1995 was inspired to buy for the school a tulip poplar tree from the estate of Franklin Roosevelt as memorial to all the townspeople who had served in the war effort. In 2006, after the tree had had a chance to grow, an appropriate stone was dedicated with the help of veterans from Lincoln and Sudbury, while a student played taps.

There was also a daily attempt to strike a blow against forgetting with the help of a "This Day in History" display in the History Department hallway, listing a dozen or so events that had occurred on that particular date back in the day. Back then, those daily event lists required considerable research, but now they are only a mouse click away. They provided a wonderful way to start classes.

THE HOLOCAUST

Before the building of the Holocaust Museum in Washington and other memorials around the country, April had been designated by Jewish organizations as a time for Holocaust remembrance. Supported by faculty, students worked together to organize annual observances for many years. Each concluded with a gathering in the History Lounge, where a memorial candle would be lit and participating students and faculty would read selections aloud from various Warsaw Ghetto diaries and then attempt to sing transliterated Yiddish songs. To keep the school community interested, the theme of the observance would change from year to year.

One year the focus was on the millions of children who were swallowed up by the Holocaust. In addition to informational posters, a stretch of barbed-wire fence was constructed near the main office, in front of which was placed a large pile of shoes—actually, old, battered sneakers of the kind that our students wore. Another year, student musicians set up by the cafeteria and played the same classical music that inmate orchestras were forced to play as Jews and other victims were marched into the gas chambers.

The following April, the focus shifted to a comparison of the human ravages of the Holocaust and American slavery. Still another year, students were asked to wear different colors of crepe around their arms, symbolic of the color-coded, Nazi concentration camp badges.

But the most dramatic Holocaust remembrance attempted to deal with a single question: "What does the number 6,000,000 mean?" This was the basis of the "Day of Six Million Zeroes." At that time, the school had a big mainframe computer, and the Computer Department staff was asked to print 6 million zeroes. They formatted the pages so that 3,000 zeroes were printed on each sheet of that old-fashioned, tracked computer paper. They said that they weren't sure how long it would take to print out the sheets.

The plan was to run this long banner of zeroes just below the ceiling on a wall that stretched thirty feet from the Main Office. When a group came in an hour early to do this, there was a surprise waiting. The printer had worked all night, producing an accordion ribbon of paper four inches thick. As the students struggled to put it up, the banner wound its way around half the school. Everyone was stunned. It is said that one death is a tragedy, one million deaths a statistic. Still, the Day of Six Million Zeroes helped to powerfully impart a sense of the Holocaust's magnitude.

SHAYS' REBELLION AND THE "BATTLE OF THE MONUMENTS"

History called out both close to and far from Lincoln-Sudbury's home at 390 Lincoln Road in Sudbury, Massachusetts. When a U.S. Survey course was being taught, for example, every year right on schedule, Shays' Rebellion would rise to the top of the lesson agenda. This dramatic event, which played a significant role in the call for a Constitutional Convention, was of particular interest to our students since the rebels fought only sixty miles down the road from the school.

The time spent on Shays was brief though. With a survey class, the teacher is like one of Woody Guthrie's Okies: always on the move and hoping to reach the promised land of California by June. So Shays got his moment of glory and was quickly left behind. On to the next stops: Philadelphia and the Constitutional Convention, the early national period, the party system, the Louisiana Purchase, and so forth.

But this time, life intervened. For history teachers, stopping to read historical markers on the highway is often a sacred undertaking, though it's an obsession that can drive families crazy. The kids may be screaming, everyone's famished, and someone, no doubt has to go to the bathroom. Still, first things first! The brakes are applied, the tires squeal, the car is thrown into reverse, and regardless of how obscure the event might be, the marker or sign gets read. It was through just such a scenario that Shays' Rebellion made an unscheduled encore appearance during one academic year.

My wife had some friends in central Massachusetts who lived many miles from the highway. Getting to their house required threading our way through several classic New England towns. We made this drive at least one hundred times. However, on the 101st return trip home in 1985, something new came into view. It was twilight and as the car approached the center of quaint Petersham, the faint outline of a monument appeared in a cornfield that bordered the road. S*creech!*

Sure enough, there was a monument in the corn. Apparently, almost two hundred years before, Daniel Shays had been defeated in that very field. But what stood out was the incredibly one-sided inscription on the plaque that was affixed to the granite marker. Bias had been cast into bronze:

In This Town
On the Morning of February Fourth
1787
Daniel Shays
And One Hundred and Fifty of His Followers
In Rebellion Against the Commonwealth
Were Surprised and Routed by
General Benjamin Lincoln
In Command of the Army of Massachusetts
After a Night March from Hadley
Of Thirty Miles Through Snow
In Cold Below Zero
This Victory
For the Forces of Government
Influenced the Philadelphia Convention
Which Three Months Later
Met and Formed
The Constitution of the United States

Obedience to Law Is True Liberty

Erected by the New England Society
Of Brooklyn, New York
As a Gift to the Petersham Historical Society

What a wonderful example of the historiographical issues—objectivity and subjectivity, perspective and interpretation—that U.S. Survey students had learned about and that make historical understanding so challenging. Might there be a way to turn this monument into an even more powerful lesson? Possibly, but it was late and a long journey home remained.

Two years passed, punctuated by occasional mulling. Suddenly it was 1987, and the 200th anniversary of the rebellion was approaching. With the now or never February 4 date bearing down, a colleague, Thom Thacker, helped to prepare an alternative plywood monument that we hoped would provide a real-life demonstration of the complexities of history both for our students and for the inhabitants of central Massachusetts.

The inscription on the alternative monument highlighted the bias of the original inscription by juxtaposing a mirror image:

In This Town
On the Morning of February Fourth
1787
Captain Daniel Shays
And 150 of His Followers
Who Fought for the Common People Against
The Established Powers and Who Tried
To Make Real the Vision of Justice
And Equality Embodied in Our Revolutionary
Declaration of Independence Was Surprised and Routed,
While Enjoying the Hospitality
Of Petersham, by
General Benjamin Lincoln
And an Army Financed by the Wealthy
Merchants of Boston

———————

True Liberty and Justice May Require
Resistance to Law

———————

Erected by the New England Society
Of the Bronx, New York
As a Gift to the Petersham Historical Society

But how could such a plywood monument and plaque be erected in Petersham? Could it be dropped from a speeding car in the middle of the night?

Luck intervened in a way that revealed the quiet but amazing surprises that libraries can provide. In the Brookline, Massachusetts, library, a copy surfaced of the actual speeches that accompanied the dedication of the Petersham granite monument in the 1920s. A further discovery showed that one distinguished speaker had registered a very diplomatic dissent to the wording of the bronze plaque. This evidence of disagreement gave us the courage to approach the town fathers and mothers.

To our amazement, they invited us and our monument to Petersham on the anniversary day. It was duly unveiled and placed right next to the original during our own brief dedication ceremony. The town's last full-time farmer, who happened to be a woman, spoke sympathetically of Shays and movingly of the hard times that were then pressing down on American farmers in the 1980s. Mr. Thacker then summarized how Shays had fared in high school history textbooks, and finally a friend and two students from Lincoln-Sudbury sang a song written for the occasion.

Remembering Daniel Shays

In this town, on this same spot,
on Sunday morn, a road of tears
we stand here to commemorate
though distanced by two hundred years.

'Twas here that Shays did meet his end,
was "routed and surprised," they say,
by Lincoln and his hired band,
but who was the hero of that day?

After the war that they had fought
to set us free, and consecrate
the rights of folk of ev'ry class,
they found their own hour had grown late.

Home they came after the war,
farmers to their farms again,
but debt and taxes plagued the way,
and rebel hopes began to wane.

Their lives were placed upon the block,
to debtors prison they were sent.
And farms? All foreclosed upon,
by courts on legal cruelty bent.

Shays' greatness turned on a single word.
"No," he said, and took up arms,
marched on and closed the courts he did—
now wasn't that the lesser harm?

Shays and his men marched these roads,
from Amherst on to Petersham;
"Law and order!" Boston cried,
but Shays did cry, "the Rights of Man!"

To all those who admire Shays,
his pluck, his courage, and his nerve,
consider the moral of this tale,
that law the people's needs must serve.

To the rich, too, if there must be,
another lesson his'try doth give,
their fate and wealth are best secured
when the poor too are allowed to live.

We thank you Pelham for this son,
who in Petersham did make his stand,
but remember too, all's still not well,
and the spirit of Shays stays on the land.

So to Petersham, this final plea,
please take the monument, on this day,
of plywood not of granite stone,
to mark our past in a different way.

The speeches completed, the dedication having been made, and the song
sung, our group then entered the town's schools to meet with students and
enjoy the homemade apple pies baked for the occasion.

On the following weekend, the annual reenactment battle was held. For
the first time, townspeople held signs rooting for the other side: "Go Daniel!"
and "Go back to Boston!" Of course, the army from Boston won the day.
That much was required by history. Ironically, the Massachusetts Militia
reenactors came from, of all places—Sudbury! Many of the "soldiers" were
the parents of my students, and they were lustily booed by the locals. We all
shared a laugh. A moment of great satisfaction came when, after the battle,
several of the Shays reenactors chose to pose in front of our monument.

Shays and his men lost the final military battle for the 200th time, but a
modest victory was won for history because of all the good discussion that
took place in school and central Massachusetts about the rebellion and the

nature of historical interpretation. From that day forward, Shays' Rebellion got a little more attention in U.S. Survey classes. The videotaped speech by that hard-pressed local farmer was particularly helpful in showing students how certain historical problems persist even if they go subterranean during this period or that.

One year, a baffled student inquired why his teachers had gone to all that trouble to fight the "Battle of the Monuments." Hopefully, the answer can be found in this book.

If there are lessons here for teachers, they may be these: check out the hallways; seize opportunities; make friends with the serendipitous; occasionally do spontaneous things; care deeply; consider yourself always "on duty"; and refuse to simply accept historical amnesia or the official skewing of history. All these things matter. Most importantly, never fail to brake for historical markers.

Chapter Seven

Joining Hands to Minds

Building a Cabin for a Courtyard

Give the pupils something to do, not something to learn; and the doing is of such a nature as to demand thinking; learning naturally results.

—John Dewey, *Thinking in Education*

Students who've been slumbering through school wake up. Those who thought they weren't smart find that they are. Those who feared they couldn't achieve anything discover they can. In the process, they build a stronger sense of purpose and self-respect.

—Sir Ken Robinson, *Creative Schools*

From the time of its founding in 1954, Lincoln-Sudbury Regional High School aspired to provide its students with a "comprehensive education." In plain English, this meant the school offered vocational electives for those so inclined. Even as late at the 1970s, there was still a working class in Sudbury. After all, it had once been a farming town. To serve kids who sought blue-collar careers, there was a wood shop, a metal shop, an auto shop, business classes, and a well-developed home economics program (where many a boy learned to cook!).

College-bound students also enjoyed these vocational electives, and there were occasional "interdisciplinary" efforts to connect the hands-on courses with more academic ones. An example was the American Crafts & Culture class where students studied U.S. history and made small crafts projects appropriate to a particular unit.

This comprehensive program began to disappear under pressures that will be familiar to educators everywhere: tightening budgets, layoffs, trying to save core offerings, changing ideas of what constituted meaningful skills (keyboarding vs. turning metal on a lathe). Additionally, in our case, a regional vocational school was built nearby. Within ten years, home ec and the business program were gone, the metal shop had become a fitness center, and American Crafts & Culture was a distant memory. Only the wood and auto shops survived.

Clearly high tech had won the day. Computers were becoming ubiquitous. Hammers and saws seemed so nineteenth century and were ready to be packed away with the stone tools of yesteryear. Thank goodness someone at Lincoln-Sudbury had the foresight not to do that. There were still things that needed to be built and students who needed to learn more about themselves by building them.

But *what* to build?

Those kayaking forays on the Sudbury River had set afloat the idea for a local history course about Thoreau; however, there was a challenge that first had to be surmounted. While few schools had one of America's greatest writers living just next door, most of our students only came to know him as 10th graders from the dry first chapter of *Walden*. How could enough interest be created to launch a course about this sauntering Concordian? Appropriately, the idea of what to build came after a summer swim at Walden Pond.

Just beyond the parking lot of the pond stood a replica of Thoreau's cabin, and the cabin's presence was transfixing. Why not build one at the school? That would certainly get students' attention. The spacious and enclosed science courtyard, surrounded by large windows, offered the perfect location for this symbol of simplicity in an increasingly affluent mini-mansion suburb. It could also be a place for students to experience solitude amidst the daily hubbub of a high school. If kids saw the cabin and wondered why it was there, so much the better. Their curiosity just might lead them to Thoreau. But how does one even build such a structure?

Fortunately, a colleague, Joe Pacenka, the school's wood shop teacher, was intrigued and teamed up to make this project happen. We faced some immediate obstacles. In an era of tight budgets, virtually no one else agreed with our assessment that building the cabin was an absolutely urgent educational priority. For three years, we applied to a variety of local and state foundations for funding and received only rejection notes for our trouble.

Year 4 arrived in 1997 and it felt like the bottom of the 9th inning, with two outs, bases loaded, and a full count. The cabin team was down by one run. Blinded by the sun, we just swung as hard as we could with our final grant application. Incredibly, the next week's mail brought the exciting news that a dying foundation set up by a conservative Chicago businessman to help disseminate Thoreau's ideas had approved Lincoln-Sudbury's entire request in the fund's last-ever round of grants.

And so, what Thoreau had built in 1845 for $28.12 and 1/2 cents, students and teachers would now replicate for a mere $12,000, using the same shingles, heavy timbers, post-and-beam construction, and traditional tools (whenever possible). Our experience goes to show that if you have a project in mind, there just might be a wonderful foundation out there that loves your crazy, impractical idea.

The initial plan was to offer a one-semester elective that would meet twice a week during our seventy-five-minute "long blocks." The cabin would be completed in the first quarter, with the second reserved for reading Thoreau's writings. Fortunately, Joe Pacenka knew how to read the National Park Service blueprints or we would have been utterly lost. We began with the class pouring a foundation and then retreated into the wood and auto shops to build the cabin frame, which would be taken apart once completed and then reassembled outdoors.

Twenty-five students signed up for what was probably one of the most heterogeneous classes in the history of the school. There were equal numbers of males and females from several grades, and every ability level was represented, from the Harvard-bound to those who preferred vocational classes.

Though we were building indoors, the class's work recalled Thoreau's own labors so well-described in *Walden*:

> Near the end of March, 1845, I borrowed an axe and went down to the woods by Walden Pond, nearest to where I intended to build my house, and began to cut down some tall, arrowy white pines, still in their youth, for timber . . . I hewed the main timbers six inches square, most of the studs on two sides only, and the rafters and floor timbers on one side, leaving the rest of the bark on, so that they were just as straight and much stronger than sawed ones. Each stick was carefully mortised or tenoned by its stump, for I had borrowed other tools by this time . . . but before boarding I laid the foundation of a chimney at one end, bringing two cartloads of stones up the hill from the pond in my arms.

Since the heavy timbers of the cabin could not be joined by nails, we found ourselves spending class periods using hammer and chisels to create tenons and mortises (a favorite project photo shows impeccably nail-polished fingers gripping a tool). This was slow and exacting labor, particularly as some students had never worked with tools before. Still, everyone gained confidence as we moved along, with the more vocationally oriented students finally getting a chance to provide leadership and guidance.

The schedule proved to be more than a little ambitious and perhaps (appropriately) utopian. The first quarter came and the first quarter went. Only by the end of the first *semester* was even the bare frame completed. *Whoops. Gulp.* As each numbered piece was joined to its mate, tenon to mortise, we realized just how much geometry was involved in Thoreau's post-and-beam design. His cabin, much like his book, came together like an intricate puzzle. Unfortunately, the bare bones of our replica were only temporarily assembled in the auto shop, and the course was . . . well . . . now over.

Building the cabin—however incomplete our efforts—had been an amazing experience. In the process, students learned about local building codes, the proper use of tools, safety issues, the importance of precise measurement, how to read blueprints, the geometry of structures, the value of close collaboration, and the taking of responsibility for specific tasks and doing them well. Thoreau did get stiffed in the sense there was no time to read his writings, but we did get to paddle canoes on the Sudbury and Concord Rivers, camp on the hill overlooking Walden, and circumnavigate the pond in the morning with a botanist who pried our sleepy eyes open.

All well and good, but what was now to come of the unfinished cabin?

Just then something extraordinary and completely unanticipated happened. Student volunteers came to the rescue. They appeared out of the woodwork, so to speak, and donated their free time by the clock-full during the school year and the following summer. By August 1998, the cabin project was finally completed. The frame was reassembled in the science courtyard, walls were constructed, plastered and painted, a roof was put on, and the whole *sha-bang* was cedar-shingled. The furniture, helpfully described by Thoreau in *Walden*, was purchased for a pittance from a used furniture store in Vermont.

But there was still one task remaining: building the fireplace and chimney. This chimney was not a task for even well-meaning amateurs. Desperate and running out of money, we called the Boston Bricklayers' Union and asked, or rather begged, for help. They were intrigued and called back to say they would be happy to help out, which they did. After three days of generously donated labor, the cabin fireplace and chimney were completed.

The cabin was formally dedicated that September. It looked beautiful nestled and protected inside its leafy, rustic courtyard home. And what a bracing fresh pine scent inside!

Though solitude is always a tough sell for teens, students in successor Meet Mr. Thoreau classes would come to the cabin for their "solitude solos" to sit, quietly reflect, and write thoughtful entries in the cabin journal (a copy of which has been preserved in the Thoreau Institute archives). What were those students thinking about in there? Here is a selection of excerpts from a number of page-long entries written between 1998 and 2007.

- I wasn't happy coming here. What was I going to do for 75 minutes in a wood cabin? As I walked to the courtyard I tried to have a positive attitude, although, yes, I can see my breath. I'm glad I came. It's totally peaceful and I definitely need some time to be alone and think. That's what this cabin provides.

- As I sit here slowly trying to let go of my sub-consciousness I can't help but be aware today is October. Summer is just slapping the hand of the fall in the never-ending relay race of time I wonder where it will all lead to— these cycles . . . We all search for what is real, search our minds for what is real.

- The first thing I noticed in the cabin was the silence. It is the most peaceful sound, or rather, lack of sound that I have ever heard. I cleared my throat and marvel as the sound of it echoing through the cabin. The beauty of solitude is a feeling long forgotten in a society. What does man really need in order to live? What is the meaning of our lives?

- The serenity of this place is truly amazing and I feel lucky to be able to do this. I have not been alone with my thoughts for a long time. In this cabin, right in the middle of the surrounding school, it's a lot clearer to me exactly how many people are worrying so much about insignificant things. Now before I head out to class, I want to say one thing that I thought about a lot sitting here. Thank you to anyone who has made a positive change in my life. I would be an entirely different person without the help and kindness of certain people.

- At this point in transition of my life I feel I need these moments more than ever because school has this ability to suck the life out of life. Days go by that are void of personal thoughts. Not thoughts on how to deal with school or where I should be going in my life—I mean those moments of reflection when I go to bed at night. I feel robbed, I feel as though moments of my life have been stolen. It's not fair to say they were all stolen by others. Sometimes the thief is myself.

- I very much doubted that coming here would clear my head and yet it seems so long ago that I was half asleep in class, my head spinning with all the things I have to do by the end of today. I now feel more aware than I have been in the past few days. It's so peaceful here, so removed from the rest of the school . . . The only direction I know is my agenda book. Every morning driving to school I passed by a certain part of the road that is so beautiful. I'd like to stop the car just to look at it. I often compromise. I am always late, so I slow the car so I can gaze without swerving. There's a hill that slopes down one side of the meadow. Usually the sun is just finished rising and the hill is lit up behind a group of trees. I think how I'd like to forget the day and walk there, but I know how unrealistic this is, how it's someone's land, how I have to get to class.

- I came in here with few expectations. I did not expect any epiphanies or revelations or any sort of insight into the meaning of life. I certainly have not yet had them . . . One day maybe some deeper meaning will be revealed. However right now I find myself unable to silence the stream of consciousness or mute the sense of urgency that always prevails in my life. I can't see the school but I can sense its presence nearby. The stress of school work yet to be done never leaves . . . Why is it that I'm already dreaming of four days from now, when I will have "finished," but accumulated even more work for the following days? Now I'm overwhelmed by my very existence. Now it's time to go. It always is.

- I have to admit I brought my iPad as a precaution, as a weapon against silence.

- It's cold outside today. I found it to be particularly difficult to accept the coming winter after such a glowing summer . . . As the world goes on, I realize that even the coldest of days are a blessing. With fall comes the most brilliant of natural colors followed by the natural purity of white. Only months later, trees bloom and creatures awake to enjoy the coming heat of the summer . . . Thank you for this cabin. Such a small structure yet big enough to free my mind to grasp a concept as huge as nature.

- I grow antsy. Apparently, the process of self-reflection weighs heavily on the perception of time. If only I could truly internalize the idea of living in the present I could achieve contentedness. I struggled to suppress thoughts emerging in relation to my plans for Friday night.

Alumni would periodically return to visit the cabin they had built. So much heart was put into it, so much determination and pride, so many screams from hammered thumbs, so many good laughs. What they could no longer see were their names so proudly signed on the beams before they disappeared into the walls.

This project has a postscript.

Sometime in the late 1990s or early 2000s, meteorologists predicted that a category 5 hurricane might hit New England. Students and staff frantically crisscrossed the school's windows with tape. What would happen to the little cabin? Joe Pacenka felt confident that if the aging school was blown away, the cabin, with its stout post-and-beam construction, would be the last structure left standing. Thankfully, the apocalypse never materialized.

As it turned out, something worse than a storm came to pass. The much-loved old school building was demolished in 2004 and a new one built three hundred feet away. The lovely sheltering science courtyard was gone, but the little cabin dodged even this bullet and still stands at the school on an island just beyond the new parking lot, surrounded by pine trees. It looks out on the waste of the automobile age and tries to peek past the new ungainly solar canopy that blocks the stunning autumn foliage of the nearby woods. The cabin now seems so very out of place. Yet perhaps the statement it is making is more powerful than ever.

Though no longer protected, the cabin has survived, patiently waiting for other teachers with a passion for our New England transcendentalists. But this account is not really about cabins—or, rather, not only about cabins. The project could have involved *anything* creative. A former Science Department colleague who became a teacher in upstate New York received foundation and Kickstarter support to create gardens in her school's courtyards. The moral of the story is to dream big. Thoreau's own words provide encouragement: "If you have built castles in the air, your work need not be lost; that is where they should be.

Now put the foundations under them."

LIGHTING THE CAMPFIRE

There is one other small crafts project deserving of mention. It was a response to the tragedy that inevitably touches all school communities. A young alumnus, a former student in the Meet Mr. Thoreau course, had passed away. He was a sweet kid who soaked up everything his high school classes had to offer but simply couldn't get it together to hand in much written work. When his apartment was cleared out, his family found a voluminous journal he was keeping. He had followed no clock, but eventually did in time find his voice as a writer.

This young man had participated in a Meet Mr. Thoreau camping trip that was idyllic—until it started to pour. He stayed out in the rain feeding the fire, keeping it going, until the weather cleared. He was at home in nature, while the rest of us were doing our best to try. He was the real Thoreauvian there that day, and the cabin was later named in his memory.

When we heard the tragic news, students helped create an artificial electric campfire that became a permanent part of the classroom. It would be lowered from the ceiling and "lit" whenever an elaborate historical anecdote needed a campfire to be told around.

Students and even courses have a history. The campfire served to memorialize an unforgettable person and one indelible moment in the life of a class.

Chapter Eight

Awakening the Muse

"Here Once the Embattled Farmers Stood"

We don't read and write poetry because it's cute. We read and write poetry because we are members of the human race. And the human race is filled with passion. And medicine, law, business, engineering, these are noble pursuits and necessary to sustain life. But poetry, beauty, romance, love, these are what we stay alive for. To quote from Whitman, "O me! O life! . . . of the questions of these recurring; of the endless trains of the faithless . . . of cities filled with the foolish; what good amid these, O me, O life?" Answer. That you are here—that life exists, and identity; that the powerful play goes on and you may contribute a verse. What will your verse be?
            —John Keating, in Tom Schulman's screenplay *Dead Poets Society*

Actually, it's the muse that awakens many children. When they fall under the spell of history, their fascination is often stoked by the vivid stories, the heart-stopping drama, and larger-than-life personalities. There are also the poems they hear or read while growing up, classics like Kipling's *The Charge of the Light Brigade*, Emerson's *Concord Hymn*, Whitman's *O Captain, My Captain*, and Longfellow's *Hiawatha* and *Paul Revere's Ride*. When the poet said, "Listen my children and you shall hear," my grade-school classmates sat up straight and listened with ears and mouth wide-open.

Fifty years later, a 225th anniversary reenactment of Revere's arrest was held in Lincoln, Massachusetts, complete with galloping horses and angry redcoats. It was a spectacle to behold and a large crowd came out into the dark of night to behold it. For many, the magic began with their first reading of that poem and was not dimmed by the many historical liberties that Long-fellow took. True, Revere didn't actually awaken "every Middlesex village and farm" and never even made it to Concord, but the poet still had genera-tions of schoolchildren galloping along, propelled by his meter and rhyme.

It's no surprise, then, that this teacher in the last half-hour of his last day as a teacher read these poems to his students. Baseball players are fond of saying that they want to go out with what brought them there in the first place.

> On the eighteenth of April, in Seventy-Five,
> Hardly a man is now alive
> Who remembers that famous day and year.

What started in the public schools of the Bronx found its way to the history classes of a town in Massachusetts. In a Twentieth Century back-ground unit, students came to understand through the poems of William Blake that industrialization not only produced new products in new ways but also transformed everyday life. In a sense, it created new people. A portion of the "Four Zoas" by Blake helped students grasp this new reality after we worked together to unlock the poem's meaning.

> The hour glass contemn'd because its simple workmanship
> Was as the workmanship of the plowman & the water wheel
> That raises water into Cisterns broken & burned in fire
> Because its workmanship was like the workmanship of the Shepherd
> And in their stead intricate wheels invented, Wheel without wheel,
> To perplex youth in their outgoings & to bind to labours
> Of day & night the myriads of Eternity that they might file
> And polish brass & iron hour after hour laborious workmanship,
> Kept ignorant of the use that they might spend the days of wisdom
> In sorrowful drudgery to obtain a scanty pittance of bread,
> In ignorance to view a small portion & think that All. And call it
> Demonstration, blind to all the simple rules of life.

Later, in the context of the Crisis of 1890, students would read "Bryan, Bryan, Bryan," Vachel Lindsay's evocative poem about the election of 1896 that so heartbreakingly captured the disappointment of his boyhood dreams:

> Boy Bryan's defeat.
> Defeat of the western silver.

Defeat of the wheat.
Victory of the Letterfiles
And plutocrats in miles
With dollar signs upon their coats,
Diamond watchchains on their vests
And spats on their feet.
Victory of the custodians,
Plymouth Rock,
And all that in-bred landlord stock.
Victory of the neat.
Defeat of the aspen groves of Colorado Valleys,
The blue bells of the Rockies,
And blue bonnets of old Texas,
By the Pittsburgh alleys.
Defeat of alfalfa and the Mariposa lily
Defeat of the Pacific and the long Mississippi
Defeat of the young by the old and silly.
Defeat of tornadoes by the poison vats supreme.
Defeat of my boyhood, defeat of my dream.

Not only was this poem wonderful to read aloud, but it provided students with a range of new information—from factual to emotional—about this critical presidential election. The poem also provided an opportunity for students to consider why such unconventional sources have to be handled with great care. The poem's subjectivity is its greatest strength and can lead us into the heart of a personal truth. But that strength can also be deceptive if it misleads students into believing the verse expressed a universal perception. Poems . . . handle with care!

Later, we would come to the better-known poetry of Langston Hughes and Countee Cullen and the other famed Harlem Renaissance poets. What textbook can take students more deeply into the emotional reality of the African American experience than these poems by Hughes?

The Negro Speaks of Rivers

I've known rivers:
I've known rivers ancient as the world and older than the
flow of human blood in human veins
My soul has grown deep like the rivers.
I bathed in the Euphrates when dawns were young
I built my hut near the Congo and it lulled me to sleep.

I looked upon the Nile and raised the pyramids above it.
I heard the singing of the Mississippi when Abe Lincoln
went down to New Orleans, and I've seen its muddy
bosom turn all golden in the sunset . . .

and

The Negro Mother

Children, I come back today
To tell you a story of the long dark way
That I had to climb, that I had to know
In order that the race might live and grow.
Look at my face—dark as the night—
Yet shining like the sun with love's true light.
I am the dark girl who crossed the wide sea
Carrying in my body the seed of the free.
I am the woman who worked in the field
Bringing the cotton and the corn to yield.
I am the one who labored as a slave,
Beaten and mistreated for the work that I gave—
Children sold away from me, husband sold, too.
No safety, no love, no respect was I due . . .

In Postwar America classes, students read Yeats's incomparable "The Second Coming" to frame the entire course and develop themes for the coming year's study:

Turning and turning in the widening gyre
The falcon cannot hear the falconer;
Things fall apart; the centre cannot hold;
Mere anarchy is loosed upon the world,
The blood-dimmed tide is loosed, and everywhere
The ceremony of innocence is drowned;
The best lack all conviction, while the worst
Are full of passionate intensity.

Surely some revelation is at hand . . .

Poems can make a lasting impression on history students. Just how lasting was made clear by this Facebook comment posted by a Lincoln-Sudbury graduate on May 18, 2018.

Thoughts on apartheid, callous government, racism, and guns in America: I remember reading Christopher Van Wyk's poem "In Detention" as part of the unit on apartheid in South Africa in my World Crises in Historical Perspective class in 1989 or 1990. Read the poem—it's powerful in its economy of words, and the way it bitterly lampoons the propaganda of the apartheid government and the cruelly careless way it dismissed the deaths of the black people it systematically imprisoned. The explanations in the poem become jumbled and rote and don't make any sense because there wasn't any sense to be made of these deaths. The subtext is that the government knew this and didn't care. I thought of this poem today in advance of the propaganda that is sure to come from our government in the US, about the nature of the deaths of the students in the school shooting in Texas this morning.

To read a poem in class or have students read it in school or at home is to engage mind and heart. It sets the table for discussion. What is the poem's meaning? What techniques did the poet use to express his or her understanding? What impact did the poem have on you? What does it add to our understanding of the topic under study? What are the limits of the poem as a source?

Given the power of poetry to stir the historical imagination, would it be possible and desirable, this teacher wondered, to require students to write their own verses about the history they were studying? Perhaps, but doesn't poetry require a lightning bolt of inspiration? Can creativity really be mandated? Such an assignment seemed forced, artificial, unfair, almost unethical. Besides what teacher needs even more papers to grade?

The school literary magazine showed just what student poets were capable of writing, so occasionally students were given the option to write a poem if a history assignment lent itself to that, or if they wished to earn extra credit. Some terrific poems were handed in by Meet Mr. Thoreau students. Here's one that was shared in the otherwise all-prose "Thoreau Cabin Journal." The student describes her experience watching the sun rise at Walden Pond:

Sunrise at Walden

Waiting
In the inky darkness of dawn
anticipation hanging heavy in the air
so thick you can reach out and touch it;
watch it slowly ripple in the sky.

Slowly, imperceptibly the sky grows brighter,
unnoticed until all of a sudden
the trees are silhouetted
against a deep velvet sky.
The fog, ghosts on horseback
galloping to some central unknown destination;
water bugs waking scamper quickly
tending to their usual business.
The lone pair of footsteps
of an unknown fisherman
amble unhurriedly to a prospective new catch.
Splash! The noise of his solitary reel
slicing through the fog.
The cars pass more frequently now,
Speaking to it a later hour;
thousands of impatient people
one after one after one
faceless headlights oblivious to
the experience they pass up every day
without ever really seeing.
Calls of birds, trucks whizzing by,
an airplane passing overhead,
more telltale signs of morning
in a semi-secret haven,
hidden from the immediate world.
The sky, glowing brightly now,
but ah! where is the sun?
Brightly burning orange ball
halfway cross the world.
The night releases
its tightly clenched fist, allowing the sun to escape,
bursting forth in all its glory . . .
Resigned to another day.

After field trips, students were usually given the opportunity to hand in poetic reactions for extra credit. This one was inspired by a class trip to New York City.

New York City

Swept across New York with the autumn leaves,
walked on Concrete Marble Granite Wood Stone Mosaic Grass,

Fell in step with the Beats
fifty years late, better late than
Never had I seen
Lennon's Park, St. John the Divine Cathedral, Ruth's Stadium

Ivied Columns and Latin Words Columbia
Tattoos Piercings Pipes Bohemian Greenwich Village.
Red Letter Lights Bulbs Forever Apollo.
Coke Cans Marlboro Lights Graffiti Bronx.

Hit pavement hard.

Blinded by taxi yellow and New York black,

Saw glass high-rise
rust railroad bridge
desolate wasteland
beauty cast in concrete and flesh.
Saw New York.

Finally, Postwar students had an extra-credit option to hand in their own life-experience version of Allen Ginsburg's "Howl." A number of the efforts were incredible, but of course the student "Ginsburgs" had the Beat poet's vision, rhythm, and structure to lean on. That being said, the students were all thrilled when Columbia University made them a part of its Ginsburg archive. They were evidence of the poet's—and the poem's—continuing influence on a new generation. Here's a sample:

Four Years of Howling

I saw best minds of my generation destroyed by madness, over-achieving hysterical
callow
dragging themselves through the blue halls at dawn looking for their first block class
voguish youths burning for the heavenly chance of a nullified seventy-five minutes
allowing access to the paved-road to Dunkin' Donuts

who weary and bored and over-conversant sat up discovering the power of derivatives
and vectors and life with rain dripping from the ceiling and the sun causing a blinding glare on the white board

who bared their brains for an A, in an attempt to swash-buckle for receiving access to the most refined educational asylum
who passed through the caf with confidence and poise envisaging uncertainty and self-worth in the web of preppies jocks druggies freaks outcasts
who were rejected from the cliques for being different & making an ideal of adherence
who fell into rooms of knowledge and integrity, tired and besieged before the administrators of their future.
What sphinx of academic adrenaline peered into their skulls and ate up their intellect and dreams?

Tests! Homework! Grades! Stop exams and the all too stressful path to College! Parents screaming on the phones! Students sobbing inside themselves!
They broke their pencils writing their explanations! Science, English, Math, History!
Raising anxiety level above the bodily amount
Real knowledge hidden by evaluation! They saw it all! The desperate eyes! Confused
generation!

Seniors! I'm with you in Last Semester;
where your laziness infects me with senioritis
Mom & Dad! I'm with you in Last Semester
where your confidence engulfs me, allowing me to still succeed
I'm with you in Last Semester
where your teaching is just as influential and important
in my dreams you walk down that platform in your cap with the tassel and the white gown, in your hand a paper signifying the four years of howling and the pride
within is infinite.

Still, pedagogical punches were being pulled. These forays into the poetic were all optional. Students took up the challenge if they chose to, but they weren't being put on the creative spot. What about putting them there?

It was now or never to attempt an experiment because time was running out on a long career. But before a teacher could reasonably require students to write a poem, wouldn't he have to see if *he* could write poetry "on demand"? During the summer of 2004, this leap into the creative ether began with visits to forgotten or presently "invisible" historical spots to see if their residual power could give this teacher's pen a friendly push across the page. It can be confidently said that no masterpieces were written that summer, but the results were sufficiently encouraging to have students give it a try.

This is how it came to be that in 2005, thirty-two years into one teacher's teaching career, the writing of poetry became a requirement in one Lincoln-Sudbury Twentieth Century American History course. The hope was that these assignments would help close the emotional distance between student and subject.

Here is how it worked. Students would be briefly shown an oversized photograph as a prompt (some of these were famous images, some not). Students would then be given a few minutes to write some notes about it as well as their reaction to it. They then had a few days to write a poem, followed by one additional opportunity to revise it. These poetry assignments were given during units on industrialization, immigration, the Progressive Era, the Twenties, the Great Depression, and World War II.

Some of the students' creative responses are included here.

INDUSTRIALIZATION

Photo prompts: Factory girls and mine boys

Grimy Windows

You look into her eyes and see

She can't live a life that's completely free
She's standing in the shadow, she's staring at death
If only she could catch her breath

She leaves before sunrise

And arrives after it has set

Darkness is all she sees, is all she knows
If only light would come

Through the grimy windows of the factory
You may catch a glimpse of her
Concentrating on her task, she never looks up

If only she could dream
She would dream of magic places,
Of wide open spaces and wide fields
Surrounded by life as she absorbs it all

If only she could be free

she stares with steel in her eyes
cutting into my skin
coal caught in her lungs

she suffocates

and the smog dims the sun

gritty hands, callused
greasy smock

blisters ailing her feet

But she is taught not to feel
her tiny hands blur into the machine
for two dull coins in which

she can barely see her reflection

she fades to black.

They Speak No Words

They speak no words,
and if they did, none would answer them.

They sing no songs,
and if they did, none would hear them.

They toll in the mines like slaves;
Wiping the dirt from their eyes
because of stubborn instinct.

They think no thoughts,
and if they did, none would consider them.

They tell no tales,
and if they did, none would admire them.

They toil in the mines like slaves;

the younger call for their mothers in their minds
because of stubborn instinct.

They repeat no jokes,
and if they did, none would laugh at them.

They hold no hands,
and if they did, none would hold them back.

They toil in the mines like slaves;
their stomachs are growling by 1:00
    because of stubborn instinct.

They cry tears
but they are soaked into the dirt on their faces.

They cry tears, O
and when they do, none will come to dry them.

A New Man Emerges

A new man is emerging,
What a strange creature is he.

He is disguised with soot,
And hangs his head low.

He has no time for family,
Only hard work is company.

A new man is emerging,
What a strange creature is he.

He comes from the ground,
Along with others like he.
Their faces are blank,

They make no sound.

A new man is emerging,
What a strange creature is he.

He is always in darkness,
And never sees the Sun.
Although part of many,
He works alone.

A new man is emerging,
What a strange creature is he.

He leads a life without any hope,
But look at all the boys . . .
Will they not be just like he?

IMMIGRATION

Photo prompts: Families and Assembly Hall, Ellis Island

For Months We've Waited

For months we've waited
my parents' dream
Pulling me away from the only world I know
The long voyage to an unknown world
Where the roads are paved with gold
Where opportunity shines at every corner
For the first sight of America
The fresh air,
But only for a moment
We then wait for hours in a long line
We wait for freedom
Like we have been for the past two years
We still wait
The new, strange language that none of my family knows
My mother begins to cry
We don't know where to go
What to do
For months we've waited
Now we are confused

My heart pounds out of my chest
Not knowing what to do

THE PROGRESSIVE ERA

Photo prompts: Woman's suffrage march; women on strike; Teddy Roosevelt smiling

Not the Same

Waking up this morning,
I knew I was not the same.

Today I had a purpose,
And a duty to all women.

Now there were no more meetings,
It was time to finally take charge.

I felt my heart beating,
And could hear it in my ear.

So, I hurried a little faster,
On the way to meet my group.

We went to the town square together,
But once out there we felt alone.

At the mercy of stares and gossip,
We were helpless.

Each of us was different,
Something had separated us from the crowd.

Each of us was trembling,
Though we tried to look calm and confident.

With fleeting glances,
We felt the ridicule of others.

Then, a new feeling came over me,
And I knew why I had come.

Standing Strong

They stand with pride,
With confidence in their eyes,
They will fight for their beliefs,
Through anything they will stand.
They will never surrender,
They will never be silent,
Their faces like steel,
The same as their personalities.
Are they not people too?
Do they not deserve
Their own rights?
Are they incapable of making decisions?
To vote, they cried,

To vote, to vote!

Big Teddy

Look at Big Teddy
Smiling up there
On top of the World he is
He lives the life of the hunt
He rides with his Rough Riders
Out across the plains
Nothing could stand in the way of his spirit
As big as he may be
He still can't hold all his cheer
Even while in office
His smile can still be seen
He leads through a time of prosperity
His Bullmoose team by his side
Still with the unmistakable grin of Big Teddy

Teddy

An Act
One Huge Act
Say the Critics
Charismatic
Pure Character
Say the Admirers

Jumps from one subject to another
Say the Dems
Equal Rights for All
Say the Republicans

The president is only six years old
Say his Foes

Dynamic public speaker
Say his Friends

"Bully!"
Says the Teddy.

THE TWENTIES

Photo prompt: Flappers dancing

The Flapper Girl

A flapper,
A young woman.
Disobeying her parents,
Smoking cigarettes,
A bob on her head.
The trend in the '20s,
The new sexual woman,
Dancing the Charleston,
Make-up caked upon her face.
She's flirty and free,
Her sexuality is flaunted,
She wears short skirts,
Her knees are showing.
She has a sense of self,
She can vote,
She wears no corset.
She is a flapper.

Wildly Electric

It was late, well past the reasonable hour,
While the young couple danced on.

Wildly electric bodies, performing once foreign motions,
Dancing closer, faster—what would their parents think?

But it wouldn't matter, for the old ones had long ago sat down,
Leaving the floor open for younger blood.

And so the pairs continued:
At once defining a generation,
At the same time defying old traditions,
Sharply dressed symbols jumping and twirling through time.

THE GREAT DEPRESSION

Photo prompt: "Migrant Mother" by Dorothea Lange

She Can Hear Their Cries at Night

She can hear their cries at night.
The hunger gnaws at their stomachs

And they slowly lost hope.
Their hearts are hollow too.

Her dry throat gasps for
One drop.
And she misses the days it used to rain.

The roof would leak, but
They really wouldn't mind anymore.
They would fall asleep to

Silent splatter.
The wind whistles across barren fields.
It matches the children's cries,

And carries despair
Into a dusty dawn.

What Am I To Do

What am I to do
I can't feed myself
I can't feed my children
What am I to do
My children stay up all night crying
Because of their hunger
And because they slept through the day to
avoid the agonizing ache in their little stomachs
called starvation

And I cry too
For I do not know what to do
The farm will soon be gone
Just like the crops

What am I to do

I do not know
But I must do something
Because no one else will.

WORLD WAR II

Photo prompts: Child sitting in bombed-out rubble in Shanghai; dropping of the atomic bomb on Hiroshima.

A Baby Sits in the Rubble

A baby sits in the rubble
waiting for someone to claim him.
A terrified look masks his face
and sadness envelopes his eyes.

Not understanding what has just occurred,
he only knows he is alone.

Looking at the only world he has ever known,
and not being able to recognize it.

The future unknown,
the past never forgotten.

Yamato Fireworks

They flash through the sky
Yet no one is cheering
They light up the sky

But it's still dark as night
Children are crying

And there are no tears of joy

The dust settles

One is left alone

Amid the chaos

Which was once his life

All is still

Even the children are quiet

"Where will we go?" they wail

Nothing changes as they wait

For life to return

To the bleak landscape

Surrounding them

What they once knew so well

Now ravaged beyond distinction

And in the background they can hear

Yamato Fireworks.

These results were nothing short of startling, a revelation. So many wonderful poems were written, and students were able to join historical interpretation to creative expression in each of them. Even with the poems that weren't so terrific, students learned something about writing with concision, and almost all showed real progress in creative writing during the semester. Why wasn't this classroom exercise attempted earlier? Such a familiar regret! With the help of student editors, the poems were compiled into a book called "Past Tense." Students later shared some of their work at an evening poetry reading held for parents and the school community.

This was quite simply one of the best, most rewarding history projects in this classroom teacher's career. It took decades to fully appreciate the truth that if teachers hold back from assigning creative challenges, they will never discover what their students can do. And their students may never have another chance to make that discovery.

Chapter Nine

Rummaging Through the Attic Trunk

*A Few Other Odds and Ends Used to Bind
Students to History*

Great things are done by a series of small things brought together.

—Vincent Van Gogh

When it comes to forging connections between students and studying the past, there should be no sense of shame. Whatever is required to please Clio, the Greek muse of history, must be done! To this end, the fun and quirky entered the classroom as well as more serious attempts to personalize the history being studied.

For years, Twentieth Century and Postwar students were promised a free dinner if five years hence they could still recall certain obscure names on the very same date they were first mentioned in the classroom. Sometimes, an email would be quietly waiting in the inbox with no message and just one of those long-ago names.

It was a deft way to say, "Time to pay up!" Many free dinners were financed with pleasure until the advent of smart phones and calendar alerts eliminated the challenge. It was fun while it lasted and it was always good to see old students, whether or not they could somehow recall the name of Tran Hung Dao, who was the Vietnamese general who organized resistance to an invading Mongol army in the thirteenth century and supposedly invented guerilla warfare.

Maybe it was also Clio who inspired the idea of creating "trading cards" for Postwar students. More probably, the light bulb went on after cleaning a bedroom closet and finding an older son's baseball cards, the ones he promised would be worth millions one day. On these colorful *history* trading cards would be printed some memorable words from the unit just completed, such as the card quoting a blacklisted writer who had refused to cooperate with the HUAC during the domestic cold war: "I stand before the tribunal of my own mind" (Gordon Khan); or another emblazoned with these unforgettable words from the civil rights movement: "Somewhere I read that the glory of America is the right to protest for right" (Martin Luther King Jr).

Students were asked—as if it were the most reasonable request in the world—to keep one in their wallet forever. Over the decades since, more than a few alumni have opened their wallets or sent a photo to proudly show some extremely dog-eared card. What's better than sharing a good laugh! How surprising to learn many years later that the City of Vancouver, British Columbia, had a similar idea for encouraging citizens to ponder powerful words. This was accomplished by placing small plaques with telling quotations at the base of trees and lamp posts. What an imaginative use of scarce municipal real estate!

Letter writing was also used as a way to suture students to the material. The content of the letter would invariably arise from class discussions. Then the letter would be cast out to see what it could catch. Often the classroom casters received no response and only joined that ancient race of fishermen that Thoreau in *Walden* jokingly called *Cenobytes* ("See-no-bites"). Here are examples of two castings that caught nothing.

The first epistle was provoked by a TV advertisement that many students had seen.

The Gap, Inc.
900 Cherry Ave
San Bruno, CA 94066

To Whom It May Concern:

   I am the teacher of a course on the 50s and 60s at Lincoln-Sudbury Regional High School in Sudbury, MA. As part of our study of the so-called "Beat Generation," my students have been reading Jack Kerouac's *On the Road*. During one of our recent discussions, an advertising campaign of your company was mentioned.

   Specifically, we discussed the ad in which Kerouac is pictured with your corporate logo superimposed on the image, along with the words "Kerouac wore Khakis." As a teacher, as students, and as occasional customers of the Gap, we would appreciate your response to the following two questions:

1) Is it legal to use the name and actual image of a deceased individual as part of an advertising campaign? Obviously, there can be no question of free consent here.

2) Assuming your practice is legal, do you believe it is ethical to use the image of this particular man to help you sell your products? After all the meaning of Kerouac's spirit and work seems so set against the materialistic culture of his time—including the centrality of "fashion trends" and even advertising itself.

On Kerouac's grave in Lowell are the words "He honored life." Did he also mean to honor the Gap? Should you have the right to suggest he did?

We would appreciate your candid response and we thank you very much for your time.

Sincerely,
Bill Schechter

The second letter was written after a long unit on the Cold War. It was a response to a *Boston Globe* column about a domestic Cold War development in the neighboring town of Wayland, Massachusetts. Its board of selectmen received our note without comment, and the *Globe* never published the copy we sent it.

October 3, 1993

To the Editor:

In her recent column in the *Boston Globe* ("Fluoride Fray in Wayland," October 3), Eileen McNamara correctly identifies the anti-fluoride campaign in that town as a vestige of Cold War conspiracy paranoia.

How fitting that campaign should be waged in Wayland! In 1954, the town fathers fired Anne Hale, a second-grade teacher, because she had once belonged to the Communist Party. The six-year veteran of the Wayland schools and popular babysitter was dismissed despite the fact that parents of children in her class expressed "confidence in her teaching ability" and that no charges of subversive acts or sabotage involving her were ever alleged. One of her colonial ancestors was Anne Hutchinson.

One can find Ms. Hale's story in the appendix of a book entitled *The Great Fear* (David Caute, 1978). It turns out that after her firing, she became an American refugee, moving from town to town and from job to job. Unable to obtain another teaching position, she worked in an SPCA animal hospital, where she was also soon fired for political reasons. It was then on to a shoe factory. For a while, she was forced to live in a basement. Apparently, she incurred heavy debts during this time. She also felt pressured to maintain her anonymity for almost ten years. Perhaps the Town of Wayland would now care to make amends, if Ms. Hale is still alive.

In the 1950s, I grew up in a progressive community in New York City. Adults were careful in their conversations. I took cover under desks in my neighborhood school. I remember well the fears generated by the paranoid crusades of that time, and I had a mouthful of cavities.

Bill Schechter
History Dept.
Lincoln-Sudbury Regional High School

Fortunately, fishermen's luck can change.

In the Fifties unit, students read articles about the supposed moral devastation caused by a shocking new music called rock 'n' roll. Of course, those golden oldie lyrics now seem quite tame and innocent. The same cannot be said, however, of some contemporary music. We sent a collective letter to the most popular local FM station in Boston asking the general manager to explain if he believed it was responsible to use a public license to broadcast music that might not be appropriate for certain age groups during daytime hours. We received a very thoughtful reply articulating a libertarian perspective that placed a heavy emphasis on parental guidance.

Jamin' 94.5

Dear Mr. Schechter:

Thank you for your letter of December 17th.

Any feedback on our programming is always a good thing. It's important for everyone to put these questions and issues in front of us (radio programmers, listeners, teachers and parents).

Ultimately, though, it's a family's decision what they watch on TV and at the movies, what they read in newspapers and magazines and what they listen to on the radio. Then there's the Internet. It's a much broader issue.

We feel a responsibility to our listeners. However, what appeals to one listener does not necessarily appeal to another, and conversely, what offends one, may not offend another. The national charts indicate the music we play is what our listeners want to hear. It's today's hottest music.

Where younger children are involved, the parents should be involved in the decision. The parents set the tone and balance for their family, we can't make that decision for them concerning our youth.

Thanks for taking the time to write your letter.

Cordially,

Matt Mills

VP/General Manager

PS: I hope you and your students continue to monitor current events.

If memory serves, a majority of the class supported the general manager and not their teacher. The misogyny and explicit lyrics that roiled our discussions sounded no more offensive to them than the early R&R songs did to an earlier generation of teens. Either they were wrong or their teacher was getting old. This point was eloquently made by a bystander who happened to be an interested eleven-year-old. When he heard about the controversy, he felt moved to participate and penned by his own hand what easily became my class's most popular handout that year.

To the MTV Generation!

Dear Post War, please excuse my dad for being such a Tipper Gore wannabe! He just doesn't understand he is stuck in the 50s and 60s. Hey, I listen to MTV 24 hours a day and let's not even bring up his TV news. If it was up to him, we would watch documentaries about the 60s and PBS till we puked.

Sincerely, Ethan Schechter

Another letter-writing opportunity came during our International Cold War Unit. The students had read complicated articles debating who or what should get credit for ending the Cold War. In two pieces, a public disagreement emerged between George Kennan, the famed "Mr. X" architect of our country's foundational containment policy, and Harvard historian Richard Pipes. The disagreement confused us, and after a class discussion to clarify precisely what we didn't understand, this letter was written to elderly and eminent George Kennan at Princeton University. Realistically, no reply was expected.

October 24, 1993

Institute for Advanced Studies

Princeton University

Princeton, NJ 08550

Dear Professor Kennan:

My *Postwar* America class is now involved in a study of the Cold War. As part of our unit, I have given students a packet of readings on the recent controversy concerning "who won the Cold War." In the packet was a *New York Times* Op Ed piece which you authored and a response to your piece, in the form of a Letter to the Editor, by Professor Richard Pipes of Harvard University [see attached for copies of both].

In your piece, you argue that the United States Government cannot, for several reasons, simplistically claim credit for "winning" the Cold War. Significant among them is the limited capacity of one major power to influence or force changes in another. Dr. Pipes obviously disagrees with you, and he asserts that your views contradict the underlying premises, and perhaps even the actual wording, of the "Containment" policy which you first delineated in 1947.

Many students noted this conflict in their essays, but did not feel they could fully evaluate this difference of viewpoint. They would like to know if Professor Pipes did catch you in a real contradiction—or perhaps only an apparent one? Or did Dr. Pipes misunderstand and inaccurately characterize your views of forty-five years ago? If not, have you now revised your views? We would very much appreciate your clarification.

We wish to thank you for your very distinguished service to your country, and for taking the time from your busy schedule to consider our request.

Very respectfully,
Bill Schechter
History Department

One morning at school, an envelope appeared in a certain faculty's mailbox with a Princeton University return address. Could it be that Mr. Kennan, a revered figure in American diplomacy, not only found the time to write but wrote as if responding to colleagues? There was not a hint of condescension in the piece, though, had there been, it would not have been misplaced. We were simply overwhelmed by the fact of his response. The letter expressed his views succinctly and told us something about the man. What a letter to treasure!

Institute for Advanced Study
Olden Lane
Princeton, New Jersey 08540
November 3, 1993

Dear Mr. Schechter:
In response to the questions put in your letter of October 24, I would say the following:

Mr. Pipes did not, I am afraid, read very carefully the "X-article" of 1947, or other of my writings of those initial years of the Cold War. He correctly cites one of the final sentences of the "X-article" but fails to mention the previous sentence serving as an introduction to that paragraph.

> *It would be an exaggeration to say that American behavior*
> *unassisted and alone could exercise a power*
> *of life and death over the Communist movement and*
> *bring about the early fall of Soviet power in Russia.*

Actually, my views on that subject were set forth in much greater detail in a further *Foreign Affairs* article (Issue 29, no. 3, April, 1951) written some three years later. All of this makes it evident that I felt that (a) we could exert a certain influence, indirectly, on internal Russian developments, but could certainly not determine them; and (b) that the best way of exerting that influence would be by the power of example, i.e., by making our society into something that would command respect and admiration abroad and would contrast with the terrible Stalinist dictatorship. Least of all did I think we would "win the Cold War" through the extreme military preparations which Mr. Pipes, as I recall it, at one time recommended.

Sincerely,
George Kennan

So even if you are a "Cenobyte," keep casting out. You may be surprised by what you will eventually haul in for your students and course. These letters extended class discussions about issues at once current and historical to people in the "real world" with strong viewpoints and the ability to articulate and defend them. These respondents modeled effective civil and civic debate and also validated the continuing importance of what was being discussed in class.

Many years have passed since these letters were written, and the world has changed quite a bit. Many fewer people today seal letters in envelopes and mail them. But digital communications—in the form of email, social media, Twitter, and blogs, for example—have given students new and potentially more influential ways to ask questions, comment on the views of others, and express their own.

The fishing has never been better.

Chapter Ten

Getting Caught in History's Web

Students, Your Family Saga Is Before You

Life is a voyage that's homeward bound.

—Herman Melville, *Moby Dick*

Family history research represents a relatively uncultivated field of endeavor for history teachers seeking ways to engage students. It is now possible to explore this dimension of history in ways that go beyond a poster of an arcane family tree that some member of the family assembled for posterity (and maybe even for future homework assignments!).

Technology has pushed wide open the doors to the archival materials that document the lives of our families and families like them. Now that bare and skeletal tree can more often develop a lush foliage consisting of actual stories to go along with the names. Genealogy has taken on a fuller meaning.

If this was a secret, it's now out. What was once the hobby of an eccentric uncle stuck in the past has become a passion for millions of people seeking a connection with their own past, perhaps to feel a part of something less ephemeral than brief mortal life, perhaps to find in history a clue to their own lives and identity.

The popularity of sites like www.ancestry.com, the fact that seven million Americans have already spit into tubes for DNA testing, the large audiences that enjoy Professor Henry Louis Gates's *Find Your Roots* show on PBS—all these testify to a continuing mass excursion into the past. What's more, online resources have made accessible the documents and stories that describe the lives of minority groups long ignored by genealogists, libraries, and universities.

How can this newly found national passion connect to high school classes?

As all teachers know and all students soon discover, twentieth-century American history does not begin in 1900. The agenda for the new century was set by changes—technological, political, economic, and social—that accelerated during the period following the Civil War. As a nation, we are still grappling with this unfinished agenda. The current controversies about immigration and industrialization (or the related subthemes of de-industrialization, re-industrialization, or automation) are just two examples.

Invariably, students find these two topics of interest. Industrialization frames the turbulent human story of early factory life, the emergence of a new class of working people, and the rise of unions and dramatic strikes. For many, immigration recalls their own family's journey to these shores.

But it was always surprising to learn how little students knew about this aspect of their history. During the Twentieth Century course's background unit, students would be asked to describe their immigration history, their ethnicity, and the ethnic traditions that were still observed in their families. Apart from a few foods or holidays, most everything that defined the cultural identity of their forebears had already been lost. This can even be true for the children of recent immigrants. Perhaps these stories were never communicated and passed along. And even in cases where they were, American society's assimilative power is formidable.

Through family history research, high school students too can try to recover and make connections with their family saga, to find their place in the story unfolding in the classroom, and to do so not only by studying history but by "doing" it. If students can stand suspense, if they have always wanted to be detectives anyway, if they would enjoy the exhilaration of breakthroughs, then this kind of research might be right up their alley.

Personal experiences can be instructive in this regard and help illustrate the utterly unlikely things that can happen when anyone probes into their past. Besides, what student doesn't like to hear personal anecdotes from a teacher! What is related here actually happened, with real-life implications for a family and a high school history curriculum.

GETTING PERSONAL

My own interest in family history began at an early age but then went on hiatus for almost four decades. When I was a child growing up in the Bronx, my parents often sent me, when too ill to attend school, to my grandparents on the sixth floor of our apartment building. My grandparents doted on me and made staying home from school an experience to be devoutly—and often—wished.

After plying me with treats, they would allow me to explore the treasured possessions they had acquired during their long lives and kept in the top drawer of their dresser. Among them was a bag of letters, all written in strange languages (the Yiddish was recognizable, but not the Russian). In response to my queries, my immigrant grandmother, Bessie Rapoport Schechter, said simply that "the letters are from my family." When she was pressed for details—as she often was—she would always answer the same way: "Why do you want to know such foolishness?" Conversation over. Until the day she died, her history remained in a closed drawer.

When my mother passed away in 1989, my father sold their New York home in preparation for moving to Massachusetts. In the midst of this epic packing, down from the attic floated a bag of one hundred strange and indecipherable letters.

Having myself arrived at middle age and being now the father of two young children, it suddenly seemed important to me that they know something of their own history, where we came from and how this story had shaped us. My father asked for my help in uncovering this history and we embarked on a decade-long project to have the letters translated, printed, and published on a major Jewish genealogical website whose goal was to re-create—*virtually*—the European Jewish communities destroyed by World War II.

RUSSIA REVEALED

As the translations proceeded, the letters slowly opened a sealed door. We learned that my grandmother had died with a great secret that she had kept even from her two sons. Why? Perhaps she felt guilty. Perhaps it was too painful. The great secret was that when she emigrated to the United States in 1913 at the age of twenty, she had left nine brothers and sisters behind in Byelorussia. We never knew this, nor much about her life in Russia.

In response to pestering questions, she did say once that she had come from Kiev, but this was not quite true. She did not live in this cosmopolitan city, nor did she even live in the Ukraine. Rather, she came from a tiny *shtetl* (village) in Belarus called Kholmech, a place so small and remote that one of her sisters described it, unsentimentally, as "the back of the beyond."

The letters detailed the travails of one Russian-Jewish family sinking ever more deeply into desperation. War. Famine. Pogroms. Revolution. You name it. The written appeals to my grandmother for help became more urgent and explicit, arriving in the mailbox of a New York household that was itself struggling for survival during the Great Depression. In the course of this project, we weren't preoccupied, as many genealogists are, with family trees. We just wanted the story. We weren't searching for anyone because surely this Russian family had perished during the Holocaust or World War II.

We completed the main part of our book, *Bessie's Letters*, as well as our Kholmech webpage in 2000. But soon we became intensely curious about what had happened to our family during World War II. We wanted to dot the *I*s and cross the *T*s and so hired researchers in Belarus to conduct interviews in Kholmech.

Elderly eyewitnesses described a machine-gun massacre of the town's Jews that they had witnessed as children in August 1941. Were our cousins among the victims? In the Minsk Archives, the researchers found a book called *Memory* that listed the names of those murdered in the Byelorussian *shtetls*, but my family was not there. What had happened to them? Were they killed later in the war along with tens of millions of other Russians as the German armies advanced toward the east?

In 2001, we posted *Memory*'s "necrology list" on the JewishGen "Shtetls of Belarus" database site. Shortly thereafter, a Russian-Israeli professor at Hebrew University in Jerusalem, Albert Kaganovich, contacted us by email. In the course of his research into the larger, neighboring town of Rechitsa, he had come across another Kholmech necrology list, this one compiled as part of a Soviet government investigation into Nazi war crimes. Our respective lists overlapped, but not perfectly. There were some new names, but our family was still not among them. Professor Kaganovich suggested that we integrate our lists on the Web, and we were happy to do this.

Three years later, on April 29, we received another email from Professor Kaganovich. He told us that while conducting interviews among Russian emigrés in Nuremberg, Germany, for a book about Belorussian communities, he had met a woman who appeared to be a relative. He had remembered certain names from our website. Emails flew between Massachusetts and Israel. Finally, we called Professor Kaganovich to make further inquiries.

Amazingly, the family that we were *not* looking for, and had only hoped to find on some Holocaust or World War II victim list, was alive and well in Israel, Germany, and Belarus.

On May 25, 2004, we called Germany and spoke to our cousins. This was the first contact we had had with this part of the family since 1935 when Stalin cut off mail service from America. When my father picked up the phone, he had belonged to a very small family, but when he hung up, he suddenly belonged to a very large one. In one hour, our personal universe was transformed.

Up to this point, *Bessie's Letters* had been a useful supplementary resource in my Twentieth Century Immigration unit. Sharing the letters with students helped to personalize the immigrant story and to provide some "Old World" background. Through the letters, they were introduced to a problem rarely discussed in the extensive literature about immigration: the complex emotional relationships between those who emigrated and those who remained behind.

The significance of my family's history research had changed and expanded into something vast. A teacher who spent his career spinning a web of history to ensnare his students now found himself caught in that same web. Suddenly history seemed far more than a subject.

My impending family reunion in November 2004 soon became a class project, with excited students advising me about what to say and how to behave. I was no less excited. When I asked, "What is the first thing you would say to long-lost relatives if . . .", it was no longer an academic question. During those days, electricity flowed through my classes. Convincing my students of the drama of historical research was entirely unnecessary.

The reunion did occur and was a most emotional experience. The completion of this history project marked the beginning of a new era for this family of survivors.

The family history period of my life was over. Or so I thought.

THE EMERALD ISLE BECKONS

After *Bessie's Letters* had been completed, but a few years before the reunion, my wife decided to research her great-grandfather Patrick Shea and her great-grandmother Brigid Walsh. They had emigrated from Ireland in the late nineteenth century and, for reasons that were unclear, had traveled on to Amherst, Massachusetts. The project involved unique challenges because Mr. Shea was illiterate and left no paper trail, and because nearly all of Ireland's census records had been destroyed during the Irish Civil War of 1922–1923. Moreover, there were hundreds of Patrick Sheas and Brigid Walshs who came through the Port of Boston during the very same period.

Truly, this was a research nightmare. Though she did find their marriage records, she could not find where Patrick and Brigid came from in Ireland, which we were planning to visit in search of parish records. As the departure date approached, she still had no idea what county we needed to go to on the Emerald Isle.

Running low on time and luck, we visited St. Brigid's Cemetery in Hadley, Massachusetts, where many parishioners from Amherst were buried. We were hoping that a clue might be found there—and heartened to see that many gravestones of Irish immigrants had been engraved with the birthplaces of the deceased.

Alas, this was not the case with the Sheas. We were back to zero—defeated and deflated! However, just as we walked slowly back to the car, my wife decided to double back to the grave. Something had caught her eye that seemed possibly significant: in front of the grave were two potted plants, one half-dead . . . but one half-alive. Who had left them?

With the help of the distant cousins who had left the plants, one piece of the family puzzle fell into place: Patrick Shea had been born in the small town of Killorglin, County Kerry. What a moment when my wife walked into her ancestral town. Transcendent! The historical gods were clearly with us because while there was a huge gap in the parish records beginning in 1861, the last page on the "right" side of the gap contained the birth record of one Patrick Shea—*her* Patrick.

A FACTORY GIRL FOUND

Later, my wife would research her French-Canadian grandmother whose forebears had migrated to the United States at the time of the Civil War. Early twentieth century census records revealed that her grandma had worked as a child laborer in a cotton-spinning factory just fifty miles from Boston.

Having learned this, "child laborer" was no longer just a term to be routinely mentioned during a unit on industrialization. Now it was a family matter. When a topic is illuminated, not only through statistical charts, secondary accounts, and even primary sources but through reference to a person with a connection to a student or teacher, it acquires a powerful resonance.

FROM ARCHIVES TO CLASSROOM

These and other family history projects took us through national and state archives on both sides of the ocean, through Mormon family history rooms and parish offices, through reels of microfilm and yellowing records. Awaiting was frustration, dead-ends, despair, but also euphoria. Details were pursued that just didn't want to be apprehended. Facts were discovered that were useless in themselves but that led to ones that were critical. How exciting it all was.

Beyond academic, it was as if head and heart were brought together in the pursuit of history. The information, energy, and enthusiasm that these projects released flowed back into the classroom. There is nothing quite like picking at the bone of history and finding that it's your own bone.

All of this is available to teachers and students, and the good news is how much more is accessible on the Internet. For example, when researching the names of the ships that brought my grandparents to Ellis Island, requests for information had to be made to a local Mormon Family History Center that would in turn arrange to have the relevant microfilm sent from Utah. Such requests could take weeks, if not months. Now much of this information is just seconds and a mouse click away.

For many students, the Internet is too often a convenient place to find cut-and-paste reports. Researching family history material, however, requires students to analyze the rich selection of primary documents and statistics available. To be successful, students must do their own detective work, learn to be persistent, figure out how to find the facts, how to evaluate them, how to use them to find more, and how to surmount obstacles and seeming dead-ends.

If successful, they will be able to put their own family—and themselves—into a wider historical perspective and to learn, in personal terms, how they are connected to the people and events of the past. Adolescents are naturally preoccupied with the question "Who am I?" They may find some answers waiting for them in online archives.

Their history is before them.

Chapter Eleven

History in the Headlines

Why Newspapers Are a Teacher's Best Friend

News is the first rough draft of history.

—Alan Barth

Families that lived during the glory days of newspapers are doubtless familiar with the common breakfast table squabbles over who got to see the sports section first. Our family survived these breakfast battles and the two main combatants—brothers—each went on to become editor of their high school newspaper. Eventually one became a professional journalist, while the other gravitated toward the history classroom and a school newspaper advisorship. For both, if even one day passed without reading the *New York Times*, the world seemed askew.

The Chinese greeting "May you live in interesting times" is intended, it turns out, as a curse. Admittedly, the post–World War II period has sometimes felt like that. But Thoreau's expressed gratitude that he was born "in the nick of time" strikes a more familiar chord. From this teacher's high school graduation on, the drama has been nonstop: the Cold War, the civil rights movement, Vietnam, the women's movement, Watergate, and on and on. No one who has even a minimal familiarity with national and international developments today would argue that our country and world have grown any duller.

It wasn't difficult for World Crisis students to understand why they needed to keep up with the latest news. They were excited to come to class and update their classmates about a late-breaking story—concerning Ireland,

Israel, Chile, or South Africa, for example—that they had just read about or heard on the radio during lunchtime. Reading newspapers or online articles or listening to other news media—and doing so critically—is a habit that schools should help cultivate, especially given the assertions of "fake news," real or imagined. After all, how can democracy thrive unless citizens are well informed?

Only later did it become apparent how valuable newspapers could be in American history classes. In fact, they help to resolve a major reason some students find history boring and pointless—namely, being forced to study a subject that seems stick-a-fork-in-it dead. Reassuring bromides about how understanding history may help us avoid making the same mistakes can go only so far. Newspaper articles can help teachers make the incontrovertible case that students are actually being required to study not the Dead Past but the Living Present. Moreover, they can see and read the evidence for themselves in a concise format.

Over the years, hundreds of relevant news stories arrived in class right on time. There were letters to the editor about particular issues (for example, immigration or foreign policy); articles about important anniversaries (the Haymarket riot or the Triangle fire); the discovery of facts that shed new light on events or personalities, ended debates, or resolved legal mysteries (the World War I armistice, Charles Lindbergh, the Rosenberg case); and reports that demonstrated the continuity of historical or analogous conflicts (the Cold War vs. the War Against Terrorism).

When we were learning about the Scopes Trial, some newspaper somewhere always helpfully carried an article about a new town or state effort to restrict the teaching of evolution. When we were discussing the origins of World War I, news reportage of the Bosnian War made history discussions—*poof!*—seem quite contemporary.

Indeed, the timing was often so uncanny that students came to believe their teacher had supernatural powers to conjure up these news clippings when needed. Unfailingly, newspapers delivered the vast world of the past and present hot and fresh to the classroom door every morning.

Here in no particular chronological order is an abridged list of articles that were used as course handouts. Some are out-of-date now and others surprisingly not. Hopefully, they provide a sense of the multiplicity and diversity of current news items that managed to pierce the present/past barrier. This is just a sampling of the bounty that the news media offers history teachers.

Old Story, New Info

- "A Wing and a Myth" [Amelia Earhart]—*New York Times*, 12/27/1996
- "New Inquiry, Old Conclusion in Huey Long's Death"—*New York Times*, 6/6/1992
- "Genetic Material of Virus from 1918 Flu Is Found"—*New York Times*, 3/21/1997
- "Ex-Freedom Rider Sues U.S. '61 Injuries"—*New York Times*, 1/23/1982
- "4 McCarthy Era Victims Compensated"—*Boston Globe*, 4/29/1982

New Historical Developments

- "Bush and Yeltsin Declare Formal End to Cold War"—*New York Times*, 2/2/1992

Parallels or "Echoes" or Analogies between Events Then and Now

- "Pagoda in Berkshires Hamlet Burns after Anti-Vietnam Phone Calls"—*New York Times*, 1/3/1998
- "71 Ohio Savings Institutions Shut for 3 Days in Effort to Stem Run"—*New York Times*, 3/1
- "Let's End Prohibition on Drugs"—*New York Times*, 3/199/1997
- "The Politics of Nativism"—*New York* Times, 1/14/1994
- "Legacy of Ku Klux Klan Haunts Indiana Town"—*Boston Globe*, 7/1995
- "In Bosnia's Schools, 3 Ways Never to Learn From History"—*New York Times*, 11/25/1999
- "In Reversal, More Blacks Are Moving to the South"—*New York Times*, 2/1/1998
- "Since Lincoln, Wartime Rights Erode"—*New York Times*, 2/14/1991
- "How Brandeis Saw Wartime Free Speech"—*New York Times*, 2/4/1991
- "Misery on the Meatpacking Line"—*New York Times*, 6/14/1987
- "Widespread Child Labor Violations"—*New York Times*, 3/16/1990
- "After Years of Decline, Sweatshops Are Back"—*New York Times* 10/12/1983
- "Three Meat Workers Found Dead Near a Tank of Blood in Kansas"—*New York Times*, 6/1/1991
- "Thai Workers Set Free of Sweatshop in California"—*New York Times*, 8/4/1995

New Evidence or Allegations Emerge about
Historical and Legal Controversies

- "Did Byrd Reach Pole? His Diary Hints 'No'"—*New York Times*, 5/9/ 1996
- "My Father's War" [World War I armistice]—*New York Times*, 11/10/ 1993
- "Photography Confirms Peary's Pole Claim"—*New York Times*, 10/10/ 1990
- "Of the Titanic and Other Man-Made Disasters"—*New York Times*, 8/30/ 1986
- "FBI Maligned Dr. King in Death"—*New York Times*, 5/1977
- "Nixon in Interview, Questions '60 Vote"—*Boston Globe*, 4/13/1984
- "1971 Tape Links Nixon to Plan to Use 'Thugs'"—*New York Times*, 9/24/ 1981
- "Facts on File" [Walt Disney identified as FBI informer]—*Boston Globe*, 5/20/1993 and 7/29/1993
- "ABA Acquits Rosenbergs with Poor History and PC"—*Wall Street Journal*, 8/18/1993
- "FBI Kept a File on the Supreme Court"—*New York Times*, 8/21/1988
- "California Newspaper Say Reagan Was an FBI Informant"—*Boston Globe*, 8/26/1985

Follow-up Stories

- "Veterans of C.C.C. Reunite in Forest"—*New York Times*, 9/11/1983
- "Temperance Union Still Going Strong"—*New York Times*, 9/14/1989
- "Capone's Vault: Inside Crime's Closet"—*New York Times*, 4/1992
- "Searching for Graves—and Justice—in Tulsa"—*New York Times*, 3/20/ 1999
- "The Day Bisbee, Ariz., Deported 1,000 Miners"—*New York Times*, 9/25/ 1985
- "Photographs Show the Titanic in Mint Condition"—*Boston Globe*, 9/ 1985
- "The Wobblies Are Back in Business"—*Chicago Tribune*, 5/28/1978
- "Islanders Remember Day They Said Aloha to Their Past"—*Boston Globe*, 8/1998
- "Where Custer Last Stood: Memorial for the Other Side"—*Boston Globe*, 9/18/1990

- "America's Dirty Little War in the Pacific"—*Boston Globe*, 2/22/1986

Eyewitness Accounts

- "Vanzetti Sister Is Still Bitter"—*Boston Globe*, 10/27/1979
- "At 93, He Still Has No Doubt: Sacco, Vanzetti Were Guilty"—*Boston Globe*, 7/31/1982
- "Jerseyan, 89, Tells of Horror of the Lusitania"—*Boston Globe*, 5/5/1985
- "Veteran Recalls a 19th Century [Spanish American] War"—*New York Times*, 11/11/1985

*Retrospective Stories about Anniversaries of Events
or the Deaths of Historical Figures*

- "Berliners Hail Togetherness and Jesse Owens"—*New York Times*, 3/11/1984
- "Joe Louis's Burial Stirs Memories of a Champion"—*New York Times*, 4/1981
- "Red Grange, Football Hero of 1920s, Dead at 87"—*New York Times*, 1/29/1991
- "A Celebration of Women's Right to Vote"—*New York Times*, 8/27/1995
- "60 Years Later, Paris Conjures Up Spirit of St. Louis"—*New York Times*, 5/22/1987
- "Police Strikers of '19 Honored by Kin, Union"—*Boston Globe*, 4/7/1998
- "Labor Marking 75th Anniversary of Triangle Shirtwaist Fire"—*New York Times*, 3/26/1986
- "For Bread and Roses: Lawrence Remembers Striking Mill Workers of 1912"—*Boston Globe*, 4/28/1980
- "Haymarket Labor Martyrs Honored"—*New York Times*, 5/4/1986
- "Shoichi Yokoi, 82, Is Dead; Japan Soldier Hid 27 Years"—*New York Times*, 7/2/1997
- "50 Year-Old Treaty [Kellogg-Briand] That Tried to Outlaw War"—*Boston Globe*, 8/24/1978
- "Remembering Jeanette Rankin"—*New York Times*, 4/1993
- "LaFollette Hailed as Governor"—*New York Times*, 1/10/1982
- "Anniversary of a Tragedy" [Kent State shootings]—*Boston Globe*, 5/1/1988
- "Germany Remembers the Berlin Airlift"—*New York Times*, 6/26/1989

- "Mario Savio, Protest Leader Who Set a Style, Dies at 53"—*New York Times*, 11/8/1996

Debates over Historical and Current Controversies

- "No Mysticism in Oz, Just the Populist Credo"—*New York Times*, 12/20/1991 [one of several articles in the *New York Times* that year debating whether or not L. Frank Baum wrote *The Wonderful Wizard of Oz* as a populist allegory]
- "Assessing Eleanor Roosevelt as a Feminist"—*New York Times*, 11/5/1984
- "The Conservation Corps Is About Jobs"—*New York Times*, 1/2/1985
- "Conservation Corp Would Hurt Workers"—*New York Times*, 12/1984
- "A Black Group Assails Statue of Suffragists"—*New York Times*, 3/9/1997
- "Historians Ready to Give Coolidge Another Chance"—*New York Times*, 12/28/1987
- "History's Been Scandalous to Harding"—*Boston Globe*, 9/29/1997
- "Actually, Prohibition Was a Success"—*New York Times*, 10/16/1989
- "Wilson Brought League of Nations Debacle on Himself"—*New York Times*, 1/20/1988
- "History Calls Events at Wounded Knee a Battle"—*New York Times*, 3/16/1993
- "Deficits Have Kept Us Out of Depression"—*New York Times*, 11/19/1995
- "Reducing Debt Has a Depressing History"—*New York Times*, 5/1995
- "Deficits Have Kept Us Out of a Depression"—*New York Times*, 11/19/1995
- "Who Really Won the Cold War"—*Wall Street Journal*, 9/14/1992
- "Rethinking McCarthyism"—*New York Times*, 10/18/1998
- "Who Won the Cold War?"—*New York Times*, 8/20/1992

Articles That Attempt to Define the Zeitgeist of a Period

- "Discophobia"—*New York Times*, 7/10/1979
- "In the 'Lite' Decade, Less Has Become More"—*New York Times*, 8/13/1986
- "The 70's—Or, Show and Tell"—*New York Times*, 12/31/1979

- "You Can Call the 1980s 'The Ugly Decade'"—*New York Times*, 1/1/1987
- "How We Felt Then and Now"—*New York Times*, 10/11/1998
- "The Boom Generation"—*New York Times*, 9/1990

These "history in the headlines" articles underscored the continuing import of the material we were studying. They defused skepticism about relevance because students could see for themselves the palpable connections between their history curriculum and their own world. Pound for pound, page for page, no curricular material more effectively supported Faulkner's assertion that the past is not even past.

While being a "chronic clipper" was a source of pride for this teacher, today's digital technology has made panning for all that gold much easier. Search engines can locate articles on any topic, and students can now receive links to them, enabling teachers to bypass the copy machine entirely.

Apart from their value in connecting past to present, newspaper articles can also help teachers sharpen students' critical thinking skills. Discerning bias and identifying interpretations in textbooks and other secondary sources can be difficult, if not impossible, for those with only limited knowledge of a particular topic. There are miles and miles of books on, say, the Civil War and whole "schools of thought" on this issue or that. News articles are more manageable because of their specificity of focus and modest length (the average story in the *New York Times* runs about 1,200 words).

By analyzing newspaper articles, students can develop the conceptual tools they will need to study history. Imagine a class working together to dissect the bias of an ostensibly objective news article and discovering that an editor's or reporter's viewpoint can be expressed—unintentionally or otherwise—in more than a dozen ways; for example:

- wording of the headline
- point size and style of the headline
- placement of the article on the page
- angle of the lead
- facts used in the story and facts omitted
- order of facts
- repetition of facts
- word choice, especially adjectives and adverbs
- sources used or ignored

- selection and order of quotations
- use of graphics
- wording of captions, and so on

These are all important details, but another form of bias is even more profound and can cause readers to miss the forest for the trees: the decision about whether to cover a story or not. The stories assigned to reporters reflect an editor's news judgment. Such decisions are particularly important when students rely only on local papers (or watch only one channel)—perhaps because they lack access to "newspapers of record." Of course, even these storied newspapers can also reflect failures of news judgment, but they generally have the resources to do a more comprehensive job.

Newspapers have been called "the first draft of history." This is true for both print and digital versions in terms of the content reported and the placement or emphasis stories are given. Articles above the fold—or at the top of the digital screen—are considered more important than those below, and, as noted, this judgment reflects an interpretation, as do all the other bulleted factors.

The use of headlines to express relative significance has a history of its own. A two- or three- or four-deck banner headline across an entire page has long signaled for the *New York Times* news of extraordinary importance. At the time of the moon landing in July 1969, our nation's leading newspaper decided it needed an even more eye-catching style for stories of *super-extraordinary* significance. And so was born a headline style consisting of a single centered line in very large type:

MEN WALK ON MOON

This headline style reappeared once again at the end of the Watergate crisis in August 1974:

NIXON RESIGNS

Most teachers will have days forever associated with some momentous news event that occurred during a school day. For this teacher, these included the *Challenger* disaster and the release of Nelson Mandela after twenty-seven years of imprisonment. But thoughts of such consequential developments were distant on September 11, 2001, a beautiful fall day at the start of a new school year.

That morning, the first Journalism class of the year was wrapping up. After the students had been told about the *New York Times'* headline innovation and how it had only been used twice in the paper's history, they had a chance to see the "Men Walk On Moon" example in an oversize book of famous front pages.

The class ended minutes later at about 8:50 a.m. As the kids flowed into the hallway, the director of the adjoining AV department was asking passers-by to step into his office to check out a developing story that was being reported on live TV. There had been a terrible accident in New York City. A plane had apparently flown into the World Trade Center.

The next day, for only the third time in its history, the *New York Times* ran its mega-headline:

U.S. ATTACKED

Suddenly, in a flash of shock and carnage, we went from studying history to trying to pick our way through it.

Chapter Twelve

Welcome to the Classroom World

Please Take a Seat

Perhaps I should give some account of myself. I would make education a pleasant thing both to the teacher and the scholar. This discipline, which we allow to be the end of life, should not be one thing in the schoolroom, and another in the street. We should seek to be fellow students with the pupil, and should learn of, as well as with him, if we would be most helpful to him. But I am not blind to the difficulties of the case.

—Henry D. Thoreau, Letter to Orestes Brownson, 1837

Any teacher who walks into the classroom for the first time will have a number of decisions to make, whether about the room, the pedagogy, the curriculum, or his or her "way of being" while teaching. Here are some approaches to consider—how they developed and why. Becoming a history teacher means mastering the material, but inevitably other issues come to the fore that will soon enough demand attention.

THE CLASSROOM

On the first day of a new career, a teacher is assigned a classroom. Usually, it is a barren affair decorated only with concrete walls and rows of standard desks. It's safe to say that "sterile" will probably more accurately describe the space than "homey." From the get-go, the new teacher is understandably preoccupied with more pressing issues: What will the students be like? Will discipline be an issue? Can I stay one chapter ahead with lesson planning? Where will I find readings and other resources?

After all, a room is a room. That's true enough until the new teacher begins to experience it as a hindrance rather than a help. Of course, the space may not be a factor one way or the other. Perhaps the potential of the room has not even been considered because of a mile-long list of other tasks that need to be addressed.

Enter Sir Winston Churchill. At the end of World War II, this iconic British prime minister explained why he was determined to rebuild the bombed-out Parliament building exactly as it had been. "We shape the buildings," he said, "and afterwards, our buildings shape us." Most teachers will decide at some point that the same can be said of classrooms.

The two classrooms that served as my main workplaces throughout a long career started as soulless cinderblock cells. That would change. Had a visitor entered them a few years later, the rooms would have appeared very different and both would bear the same aesthetic fingerprint. It would not have required a skilled forensics team to conclude that the very same guy had decorated both.

The visitor might have been taken aback at first to see that every inch of the cinderblock acreage had been given over to colorful historical and political posters, famous photographs, large blow-ups of significant newspapers, and provocative quotations or statements about history. Clearly this was a place where blank walls were considered anathema and a waste of precious real estate.

The posters and prints were conscripted into the cause of beautifying and historicizing the space, perchance to do a little teaching of their own. Some colleagues must have found this "total immersion" aesthetic excessive, distracting, and over-the-top. They clearly preferred to teach surrounded by silent walls, perhaps believing that a quiet canvas was the best way to focus a class's attention.

There is no right answer here. Classroom decoration is a matter of personal choice, but it should be a deliberate one. Certainly an argument can be made for mobilizing the physical environment in support of one's teaching. Besides, if the teacher isn't cutting it on a particular day and a student's attention happens to drift to a poster or a quotation, then all is not lost. (It was always surprising—and gratifying—to hear students or alumni call to mind a quotation or poster that had made an impression on them during the school year.)

In the spirit of authenticity, this one caution is offered: prefabricated, processed, insipid materials sold by education supply houses should be avoided. Better sharp aged cheddar than Kraft singles.

Decoration can help create a stimulating learning environment, but how the classroom is physically organized is more important because the arrangement chosen can encourage—or discourage—student interaction. A number of colleagues at Lincoln-Sudbury had arranged their room in way that seemed very helpful in facilitating a participatory pedagogy. They had students sit at desks or tables lining three sides of a rectangle, which signaled an interest in having discussions because classmates could actually see each other. As for this teacher, his chair was placed on the open side, but with all the tables drawn as close as possible, because distance creates . . . distance.

A sense of informality was also created with the help of a few beanbag chairs scattered in the open space in the middle for those who preferred to be part of the "beanbag community." The teacher's chair? An old rocker. While history burned, he rocked. Actually, the initial decision to sit down in class proved to be a pivotal career decision.

FINDING A WAY OF BEING IN THE CLASSROOM

Most teachers are influenced by suggestions mentor teachers make during their practicum, such as stand up at the blackboard (later whiteboard), write notes, and occasionally walk about. In most education school programs, teachers-in-training are encouraged to be dynamic and move around the classroom. This doesn't work well for everyone. It can turn a teacher into a stage performer with an audience *out there*. Equally disturbing, one's voice can begin to sound different. It can become detached, didactic, and professional, even a bit schoolmaster-*ish*.

On one otherwise unremarkable but tired day, at a moment lost to history, somewhere early in the second decade of this teacher's career, something significant happened. A chair beckoned—and the invitation was accepted. The simple act of sitting made a dramatic change. Almost immediately, students—as well as the speaker—heard a familiar voice with a conversational tone. Henceforth there was less talking *to* and more *with*. Be assured the teacher remained the teacher. The captain of the ship had not been deposed, but as the "me/them" chasm became a little less yawning, it became easier for students to participate.

Suddenly, there was a greater congruence between the person outside the classroom and the teacher persona within it. During the academic year, students would get the whole enchilada—in other words, the passion, the wisecracks, the enthusiasm, the occasional moral outrage, the wit, the New York accent, the unflagging loyalty to the Yankees (in Red Sox country no less!), the "curmudgeonliness," and always the sense that what we were doing was important. Teachers of the World, you just might want to try sitting down!

CONSIDERING THE ROLE OF THE TEACHER

When I wasn't facilitating an activity, my teaching style evolved into a "modified lecture." Classes would typically begin with a group exploration of the topic of the day accompanied by questions directed to the students. Some of these queries sought out factual answers, others interpretations or opinions, still others moral and ethical judgments. Sometimes the questions came from students who now felt more comfortable to ask them.

Sitting in a circle (or rectangle) of learners softened the edges of the lectures and helped them to more naturally morph into stories, while student responses to the queries grew more organically into both planned and unplanned discussions.

Hold it, was the word "lecture" really just used?

That word "lecture" is avoided in progressive educational circles as well as the practice it connotes: a teacher forcibly depositing coins of knowledge into a student's mental bank account, where the sums are passively received and (hopefully) processed. Some technology enthusiasts would also be dismayed by the idea of students receiving knowledge from a source other than an illuminated screen. To clarify what every teacher learns soon enough: educators can't talk to their classes all the time and students can't be relegated to taking notes. (And, yes, students did take notes. It's an important skill. How much you can tell about how students think, understand, and organize information from their notes!)

As part of a mix of pedagogical approaches, the modified lecture has its uses. Most teachers steeped in history can make the material more interesting than any textbook. It's not really a high hurdle. And even with textbook and supplementary readings—assuming the reading assignments are completed—the teacher has to be there to reinforce, clarify, elaborate, and provide context.

Teachers can and must be more than "facilitators." They have to bring their whole selves into the classroom. As has been suggested earlier, memorable lessons require a human voice, whether in the classroom or in documents. And the voice, mind, and heart of the committed teacher have not yet been rendered expendable by either group work or digital technology. Again, recalling the most memorable experiences from one's own years of schooling will affirm this truth. Why do we still remember certain teachers, classes, and lessons? Is group work on your list?

In addition to modified lectures, pedagogical variety can be (and was) introduced through structured and unstructured discussions, or discussions disguised as debates and simulations. Many lessons can be dramatically improved by attending to small details. For example, it's best to give students a few minutes to jot down some ideas first before beginning a discussion. Too often, we ask students to be thoughtful without giving them the time to think.

MIXING IT UP

The pedagogy described in this chapter made for successful lessons, but other colleagues who were very highly regarded went about their teaching very differently. Clearly, there is no "one best way" to set up a classroom or to teach. Here is an example. One colleague actually did lecture the entire period—that is, *lecture* in the old tradition!

As a young teacher, beguiled by the experimental new concept of the "democratic classroom," this approach caused much contemptuous shaking of the head. But the office window into the classroom told another story. Students were seen laughing. Then a few volunteered how great the class was. With an ear pressed to the wall to get a better sense of the magic going on in there, this doubting Thomas heard some wonderful anecdotes and stories that he immediately "borrowed" for his own classes. A respect and tolerance for different teaching styles grew considerably after that.

The challenge for teachers is to find a style that fits them and utilizes their strengths to the best advantage. The watchword is "Be Yourself." Most teaching styles can work well, assuming the teacher knows the material; prepares; develops pedagogical approaches (subject to continuous revision); cares; and provides sufficient structure, organization, and space for students to think and participate. There's no one way, but humor and spontaneity will help no matter what path is chosen.

The students will let you know in a timely way if your teaching style and lessons are effective enough. If a teacher sees students' heads drop on their desks, it's time to rethink the approach, talk to colleagues, and maybe visit other classrooms.

CURRICULUM—AND MAKING IT "FIT"

Teachers at schools like Lincoln-Sudbury, where the faculty was spared assigned course scripts, were fortunate indeed. Academic freedom was given and creativity respected—even welcomed. We had the exciting opportunity to create new courses, which, of course, also meant more class preparation and more work. That was the price of the excitement. With multi-section courses, teachers might work collaboratively in small groups, but when it came to "singletons" or new courses, we usually worked alone and had to find our own way to prepare curriculum. This was a career-long challenge, and the tweaking never ended.

As for "fitting" the curriculum into the time available . . . well, that was a constant struggle, more for some than others. There were colleagues who had every day planned out from September on. Their organizational abilities were awe-inspiring, but locking in the syllabus to that degree can also have its downside. The life of a classroom is unpredictable. There will inevitably be unexpected diversions because of a question a student asked or a discussion that couldn't be abandoned or a story that appeared in the morning paper—and off we'd go. Shortsighted though these judgments may have been, sometimes it just seemed more time was needed to honor the complexity of a particular topic.

Still, thinking ahead can only be helpful because holidays, snow days, and mandatory assemblies are always waiting to ambush even the best-laid plans. The first month of school is like a slow hike. Anything and everything seems possible. But before you know it, you find yourself racing down the Autobahn of the school year. In a school, time is the coin of the realm and there always seems to be a budget shortfall.

BREADTH OR DEPTH?

There's a simple rule in this curriculum business and it admits to no exceptions: the deeper the teacher's historical understanding, the greater the possibility for creating rich curricula, even if the former does not guarantee the latter. There's also this truism: even the richest curriculum has to balance depth of understanding with coverage of material across the year. Teachers want to cover content, but we also want to develop the material in a way that involves and captivates students. Getting that balance right isn't easy because history is fathomless.

Educators constantly find themselves wrestling with the question of what constitutes *meaningful* coverage anyway. If a teacher covers the 1920s in a day or a week, can that really amount to much more than teaching vocabulary and reducing history to "five facts and a cloud of dust"? Every day, week, and semester this issue keeps intruding, while the cruel classroom clock ticks on.

The inclination of most history colleagues at Lincoln-Sudbury was to go vertical as much as possible. The thinking was that this approach better provided students with opportunities to develop conceptual and critical thinking skills. Students also seemed more likely to get hooked on the content through deep dives into the material. The questions and problems that most engaged them were more likely to lay in the depths, not the shallows. It was down there they discovered history as contested memory and argument, as a repository of issues and perspectives that continues to roil our politics and culture.

But as with any course decision, a bill will come due. Studying themes, sources, connections, and conflicting interpretations takes time.

Getting just the right balance between breadth and depth is near impossible, but the continuing challenge can't be ignored. It's one of those goals that recedes just as teachers think they are approaching the horizon of perfection. Educators have to accept that not every lesson they teach will be mistaken for a Vermeer masterpiece. Still, genuine interest, a touch of passion, and a healthy dollop of curiosity will cover a multitude of curricular or pedagogical sins.

ASSIGNMENTS

History courses provide an opportunity to think, to develop "habits of mind," and to learn how to write. Our department prided itself on assigning more writing than the English Department, or so we liked to believe. In Twentieth Century and Postwar classes, apart from some worksheets that accompanied textbook readings, students answered a few questions about every reading they received, wrote occasional three- to five-page essays, and completed both a six-page and a ten-page term paper. Students learn to write by writing and doing so with encouragement and constructive criticism. The term papers were a culmination of the various skills they had learned during the year: conceptual and critical thinking, analysis, organization, reading with care, writing, and research.

Graduation tests for apprentice bricklayers often involve building a perfectly plumb wall, and term papers present a comparable challenge. Teachers need to see that ambitious student work is straight and plumb. Occasionally, alumni would write to say what their term papers had meant to them or how it connected them to some current project or interest.

All this writing translates into a whole lot of grading. If, after a long career, a history teacher has not developed back problems, he or she is probably doing something wrong. (Of course, the number of readings and assignments, and their relative difficulty, can be adjusted according to the grade and ability level of the students in the class.)

MATERIALS

For a number of years, the invention of copy machines worked a revolution in teaching, enabling those of us so inclined to give students a greater variety of materials than just a textbook. When possible, "handouts" were bound to help save paper, with one volume for at-home readings and assignments and one for in-class with brief readings, documents, poems, songs, and primary source accounts. Still, a textbook occasionally proved useful in providing a narrative thread, names and terms, and to serve as a counterpoint to the interpretations of other readings.

Other materials included novels, with at least one required in each course, and history video documentaries—a whole film or some clips. These had become an art form by the 1990s. A comprehensive slideshow that took years to assemble—and which today might only take a few days to compile on a computer—helped students review the unit's material before an exam. Students enjoyed those slideshows and said they found the visuals helpful in jogging their memory and connecting facts to memorable images.

It may be that Clio reserves a special curse for teachers whose hubris pushes them to try to understand it all. Learning more means accumulating more and more material and having more complexity to impart. This dynamic began to clog up the pipes of a certain teacher's curriculum. One solution to the time crunch was to write mini-textbooks about topics ignored by the textbook but that had taken valuable class time to present. Now this material could be assigned as readings and so more time could be freed up for discussions. These mini-texts helped to clear out some brush, important curricular brush though it was!

MAINTAINING DISCIPLINE EVEN DURING REVOLUTIONS, RIOTS, AND WORLD WARS

In the classroom world, every teacher has to deal with discipline, or "management issues" as the topic is delicately referred to. At Lincoln-Sudbury, most students were motivated and well socialized. But kids will be kids. In any given year or class or lesson, order needed to be maintained. It didn't happen automatically. At Lincoln-Sudbury in the early 1970s, newly minted educators were often assigned to teach in what was called the CORE Program, geared to students with serious behavioral and academic problems. Each class was limited to five to seven students because otherwise classes would have been unmanageable, especially for a young teacher just starting out.

Other "beginning" classes consisted of freshmen history sections that provided a stark demonstration of the wide range of maturity within the same age group. The ninth graders were all over the place, physically and emotionally. Some were more like junior high kids, while others were closer to sophomores. Different species of adolescents were packed into the same room.

How best to impose discipline was a mystery back then. Couldn't we all just avoid the whole unpleasant subject by simply being nice? How delusionary a dream that proved to be. After one particularly difficult day, a colleague shared a valuable and never-to-be-forgotten insight: "Someone will be in charge of your classroom," he said. "The only question is who."

Out of necessity, the standard repertoire of classroom management techniques was quickly mastered: moving kids to different seats, threatening to send them to the "office," speaking to them after class, losing my temper (when all else failed), etc. These strategies were like bailing wire that sometimes helps hold things together.

But threats and intimidation have a short shelf life and they are often counterproductive. If these are the tactics that a teacher will be relying on, it's going to be a long year. Whole books have been written about how best

to maintain classroom discipline, but here are a few guiding principles that
have proven useful.

- Be direct, fair, firm, and calm.
- Humor can help, but you must know your class. With some groups, it's
  easy to fool around; with others, jokes can trigger avalanches.
- Be generous with compliments. A student once said about a heavily
  marked-up paper, "Thank you so much for all the corrections, but did I do
  anything good?"
- Be a person and role model, not a role. That means trying to be wise,
  warm, and compassionate when possible.
- Where discipline is concerned, consistency can indeed be, in Emerson's
  words, the hobgoblin of little minds. Students need different things. Give
  each what he or she actually needs.
- Try not to embarrass students in front of others. If reprimanded in front of
  friends, they may feel the need to save face at your expense.
- Calling parents can help, but realize they are not always on the best of
  terms with their adolescent sons and daughters. Teachers may actually be
  getting the most scenic and sympathetic view.
- Be prepared. A student once said that one thing she really liked about class
  was the way there always seemed to be a plan for the period. Plans enable
  a teacher to move seamlessly from one part of the lesson to another. Her
  comment was received less as personal praise than as an insight into what
  students need and want. In an effective lesson, there's no time provided
  for anyone to chat (much) or misbehave. The teacher is busy and the
  students are busy. Chatting tends to pop up in the interstices.
- When students are interested in the material, their behavior improves.
  Alas, the burden is always on the teacher to keep the customers happy.
  The challenge of keeping order diminishes as curriculum and pedagogy
  improve.

After a decade's worth of experience in the classroom, it only took a look to
cut off misbehavior at its knees. It wasn't "Joe, stop misbehaving or I'm
going to send you to the office!" It was "*Jeez*, Joe, you're truly killin' me. I
just don't have time for this. Let's turn to page twelve right now. Joe, please
read the first stanza of that poem. Hey, great job." Problem solved. No
momentum lost.

The inherent interest of the material and a culture of classroom participation helped make discipline mostly a non-issue. Additionally, the in-class and out-of-class relationships established with students were essential in helping to maintain order and harmony. Those relationships were also the most enjoyable fringe benefit of the job.

BIAS

This classroom issue was intentionally left for last because it is such a vexing challenge for the history teacher. Bias is . . .

No, this topic really needs its own chapter.

Chapter Thirteen

Bias Buzzing Around My Head

The "No-See-Ums" of the History Classroom

> The absence of falsehoods does not necessarily add up to historical truth.
> —Christopher Lasch, *World of Nations*

Bias always seemed like those black flies encountered in the Maine woods on a humid summer day. There was no brushing them away. They owned the outdoors. So while the problem of bias has been broached earlier in this book, more needs to be said.

First off, let's define terms because the word is used in different ways. In a colloquial sense, "bias" is often used to connote a viewpoint that is intentionally and unfairly skewed to support a political position or other strongly held opinion. "You are so biased!" is a familiar retort. The other meaning is more neutral but suggests we all view reality from a certain angle, much as a woodworker cuts a board on a bias, an oblique line across the grain.

Even when history teachers try their hardest to be fair and balanced, they will find themselves tangling with this issue. Bias seems baked into the subject matter, and there's no way to escape dealing with it except by being unconscious, unaware, or uncaring about the way one's own perspective inevitably shapes a course of study.

Teachers all have a syllabus—a piece of the past—that they are assigned to impart. How much of that will be taught and from which class, race, ethnic, and cultural perspective? Which topics will be covered, which left out, and what questions will be asked? What readings will be assigned? How much time should be spent on each unit? All of these questions (and, ulti-

139

mately, decisions) are loaded and fraught. As faculty, we should always strive to get things right, fair, and objective but also to understand that complete success will be unattainable. Perfection is too slippery and elusive. Perhaps the Talmud explained the difficulty best three thousand years ago: "We do not see things as they are. We see them as we are."

One would think that being forced to adhere to a mandatory state curriculum framework (the foundation of a standardized testing program) might solve the problem or at least provide a measure of curricular certainty for the bedeviled teacher. More often than not, however, these frameworks only intensify the problem by creating an official or mythological version of the past hammered out on the forge of legislative deal-making, popular prejudice, and special-interest lobbying.

In November 2014, Fox News reported that the Texas Board of Education had finally voted to approve new history textbooks for use by the state's five million students. The approval followed many hours of "testy discussions" in which seven other texts were either rejected or withdrawn despite efforts by desperate publishers to make late edits.

According to Fox, this long and heated debate was provoked by lessons that according to some academics exaggerated "the influence of Moses in American democracy and the Founding Fathers, and negatively [portrayed] Muslims." Some liberal academics also felt the texts went overboard in praising the free market system.

The Republican majority on the board refused to allow more time to vet the issues. Thomas Ratcliff, the chairman of the board, stated that the books "are not perfect, they never will be." In a straight party-line vote, all ten Republicans on the board voted to approve the books, while all five Democrats voted to reject them.

A year later on November 19, 2015, the *Christian Science Monitor*'s reporter Story Hinkley covered another Texas textbook debate that went national. This time the controversy was sparked by references in the texts to African slaves as "workers." It didn't help matters any that the board had rejected any fact-checking by university scholars. A group named the Texas Freedom Education Fund had also highlighted what they considered biased statements about the virtues of segregated schools and the un-Americanism of Affirmative Action.

The president of the fund, Kathy Miller, claimed that a number of the textbook passages reflected the ideological preferences of board members rather than a scholarly commitment to factual history. She characterized the textbook adoption process in Texas as a "clown show."

In Boston, a conservative think tank, the Pioneer Institute, has been pushing for the state to add another graduation requirement in the form of a high-stakes history/civics exam, which they would doubtless be happy to help shape. They feel only a standardized test can establish the importance of historical study and are particularly determined that all high school students read the challenging prose of the *Federalist Papers* to gain a better appreciation of Madison's argument for limited government, which just happens to lie at the heart of Pioneer's mission statement.

In Texas and elsewhere, government-approved versions of the past can easily morph into systematic indoctrination. The fact that this is exactly what Radio Free Europe criticized about the Soviet education system during the Cold War seems to have been lost somewhere along the way. Presumably an official bias is fine when it's *ours*, hence it goes by a different name: objective, testable truth.

Again and again we seem to find ourselves in a national tug-of-war with the past. On August 3, 2017, WBUR, one of Boston's public radio stations, reported that replicas of two of Columbus's ships making their way through the Great Lakes on an educational voyage had sparked protests by Indian tribes, among others. The protesters were demanding that the full story of the Columbian legacy be told, including deaths from infectious disease, massacres, and enslavement.

The *New York Times* reported on August 6, 2017, that professors on the right and left had received death threats on social media because of their writings on political and racial issues. Just as recently, 150 years after the Civil War, Southern cities are being roiled by the demand that Confederate memorials be removed. At least half of the American people think it's acceptable to memorialize rebels and slave owners in public places of honor. The other half of their fellow citizens find that practice abhorrent.

Political feelings are running high to say the least. Historical issues—and their modern analogues involving immigration, the role of government, prejudice, women's reproductive freedom, and others—continue to divide the country. And who could remain oblivious to the debates, disclosures, allegations, assertions, attacks, and counter-attacks concerning bias that have saturated the nightly news since the election of Donald Trump in November 2016?

The dance between historical understandings and politics—always an intimate one—has become a suffocating embrace in these polarized times. As a nation, we have progressed from differences over the interpretation of historical facts to denial that facts are facts or to claims that some news is nothing more than "fake." This doesn't even include the actual fake news disseminated by bots and "bad actors." Do our interpretations of the past lead us to our respective political party perspectives, or do our party allegiances determine which historical and TV news narratives we prefer?

How can one feel anything but empathy for the generations of history teachers to come? They will need to pick their way through a minefield that no teacher has ever had to confront.

Whither? Bias cannot be avoided in teaching history. Teachers will continue to make choices and decide what topics are most important. They will apportion class time accordingly—to the extent they are free to create their own curriculum. They will continue to ask questions this way or that. Use these words or those. What *can* be done is for teachers to take the time to discuss the issue of bias with their students and strive to be as honest as they can be about their own.

Sometimes teachers are not open about their biases. Usually they aren't trying to be deceptive. It's just that time is limited and, besides, they simply might not be aware that their views are contested. A respected colleague once pronounced with authority that the abolitionist John Brown was insane. After all, didn't Brown think God was speaking directly to him? Actually, the question of whether Brown was a madman is one of the most debated issues in the many works of fiction and nonfiction about him. In an essay defending Brown, Thoreau actually compared him to Christ. This colleague probably thought he was simply stating an uncontested fact. The trap of facile assumptions has ensnared me many times.

An early handout used in U.S. Survey classes consisted of a sheet of Lincoln quotes strung together in a way that suggested he was a political fraud. The mere memory of this sheet is cringe-worthy. Learning more made possible a much improved handout that presented the Great Emancipator's views on slavery and African Americans in context, which is to say, in a fairer, more accurate, and more complete way.

If a certain amount of bias is unavoidable, teachers must still aspire to a high standard of fairness. Students need every opportunity to explore both sides of an issue and, when necessary, all three or four sides. History classrooms must welcome the chorus—and sometimes the cacophony—of voices that echo down through time.

Our students need to hear from the elites, the leaders, and the presidential administrations. But they also need to hear from Native Americans, immigrants, farmers, workers, and the enslaved. A true history of the American people must go from the mountaintops to the grassroots, from the seats of power to the seat of the pants.

Evaluating and trying to reconcile these different perspectives and interpretations are what set minds in motion. The teacher's job is to use questions and exercises to ratchet up the intellectual tension in the classroom and generate thoughtful, intellectual disquiet. Teachers and students who want to discover the truth can never be part of a get-along gang. We never want heads on the desk, but some squirming in the seats induced by a difficult question is always welcome. The passions of the 1960s fitted this teacher with his own ideological spectacles when he first stepped into the classroom. The Vietnam War was grinding endlessly on and bombs still rained down a half a world away when Postwar's Vietnam unit began. Maintaining a clinical objectivity while teaching about America's (then) longest war was very difficult, and that's putting it mildly. The release of the Pentagon Papers didn't make things any easier.

Speaking from personal experience, when teachers are completely immersed in their own worldview, their own bias becomes almost invisible to them. Gaining some distance from the turbulent times of one's youth and opening the classroom door to controversy, including perspectives that seem distasteful, inconvenient, or just plain wrong, greatly improves students' learning experiences. It is exciting for kids to discover that history is studded with different viewpoints and that finding the facts, placing them in relation to each other, interpreting them, and reaching conclusions is a daunting challenge. Nothing gets handed to you in history.

Experience made this teacher wiser. Personal views were held in abeyance unless a student asked, and even then, radio silence was maintained until the students had had a chance to work through the material and issues. Because of the historiography they had studied, they were able to understand that their teacher's views represented but one interpretation and were not the infallible pronouncements of an authority figure or grade-giver. That's progress.

A final thought. Many years ago, a professor friend said something about this nettlesome topic that has remained vividly in mind. "Bias," she said, "may inform the questions you ask, but should never determine the conclusions you reach."

Chapter Fourteen

Charting a Course

One Way to Develop History Units

Plans are nothing; planning is everything.

—Dwight D. Eisenhower

A course can run through a school year like a highway or flow through it like a river with occasional meanders. The latter metaphor better describes Postwar and Twentieth Century courses because of a pedagogical inclination to organize units in the way streams lay down sedimentary layers.

Fabulous lesson plans are for teachers to create. But here is an overview of how one teacher went about planning units in two different history courses. There are many ways to develop curriculum, and all involve a thoughtful, intentional process. Of course, it goes without saying that a well-framed question can be the equal of any lesson and can even *become* the lesson.

First, start with getting the lay of the historical landscape. This orientation is acquired though reading articles and books and moving from timelines to content to analyses to anecdotes. What's true for students is equally so for teachers: there are no shortcuts. It just makes sense that the more an educator knows, the more accurate, versatile, and creative he or she can be. A good way to begin is with the "marinating" stage. Being steeped in the content will help teachers formulate better questions, explain complex events more clearly, and share more telling and evocative anecdotes that can provoke thought, curiosity, and even laughter or tears.

Second, survey all the supporting materials available: readings, videos, primary documents, newspaper articles, novels, and textbook chapters. Some of these resources may become central to your class lessons, while others will serve as valuable supplements. This is where planning also begins on where the materials will be read: at home or in class. All readings—including text assignments—will require the preparation of accompanying questions to ensure the readings are read.

Third, identify and analyze the enduring interpretive conflicts and continuing issues—historical, political, cultural, and ethical—for how they might best be explored, whether by discussions, modified lectures, various in-class exercises, or perhaps in essays or other writing assignments. In short, this is the stage where the teacher creates a "menu" of pedagogical options and then determines which ones will best develop the unit's narrative and embedded issues in the most effective ways.

The learning activities selected—lectures, discussions, readings, videos, formal debates, or elaborate simulations—will serve as the tools to crank up the intellectual tension in the classroom, to encourage participation, and to motivate students to think about the questions history has bequeathed to us.

Besides considering learning and teaching strategies, this is also the point where the rubber meets the road and decisions are made about how best to deploy the resources that have been identified. Should that newly discovered, evocative poem be part of a homework reading packet or handed out in class and read aloud to lay the groundwork for a discussion? Should those interpretive articles be tied to a few reading questions or serve as the basis for an extended, reading-based essay?

Fourth, finalize the most logical, helpful sequence for lessons and schedule lectures, discussions, group work, simulations, and so forth accordingly.

This four-step process is one of many efficient and reliable ways to approach course planning, an effort that will forever require tweaking, rearranging, and adding (or subtracting). However, no matter the method a teacher chooses, one fact is indisputable: *Teachers with only chronology to impart, along with a few basic terms for students to identify, will not be able to generate creative lessons, inspire curiosity, or encourage critical thinking.*

Self-education is a career-long undertaking, and there will be hard reminders of how much there is to know. Particularly painful is the sense of disappointment that comes when an inadequate understanding results in a confusing or inaccurate presentation. Let's always take to heart those words of Beckett to "try again . . . fail again" but "fail better." There is no escaping this law of academic gravity: engagement with the material must begin with the teacher. Only then can it radiate to the students. When King Lear proclaimed, "Nothing will come of nothing," he was stating a brutal truth. The best school cultures communicate high expectations of teachers as well as students. Respect for teachers and academic freedom doesn't give a faculty member license to enter his or her class without a daily plan or an overall blueprint for the unit—quite the contrary. Students do notice.

Here are some specific examples of unit planning that illustrate the general process described above.

COURSE: TWENTIETH CENTURY AMERICAN HISTORY

Unit: The Great Depression

Long about November when we were all "growing grim about the mouth" and crawling toward Thanksgiving break, the Great Depression unit would come along like clockwork. It's not a cheery story. It is also a sprawling topic that can easily swallow an entire year. How to handle and shape this subject? These are the topics and issues that seemed most important for the students to know or think about.

- Political Philosophy: The "Proper" Relationship between Government and Citizen
- The Immediate Political, Social, and Economic Background of the Great Depression
- The Factors That Caused the Great Depression: Why Did It Happen?
- The Growing Social Crisis of the Great Depression, the Personal Consequences, and the Immediate Government Response (or Lack Thereof)
- The Moral Issues Raised by the Great Depression: Who or What Was Responsible for the Mass Suffering? (see *The Grapes of Wrath*)
- FDR and His Background
- The Campaigns and Election of 1932
- The First New Deal: Major Legislation and Court Decisions
- Conservative Opposition to the New Deal: Who, What, and Why
- The Second New Deal
- The Political Spectrum and the Election of 1936
- The "Roosevelt Recession" and Keynesian Economics
- Evaluating the New Deal: Was It a Success?

At first glance, this is not the kind of material that will get students jumping up out of their seats to dance the tarantella, but most of them will at least concede the importance of the unit. This gets a teacher a free pass to the next day. The question is how to breathe life and excitement into a unit that is top-heavy with an alphabet soup of federal acts and agencies that, it must be acknowledged, *are* important and attract the lightning of many current political debates.

Fortunately, the time period involves far more than even a great president and an activist Congress that passed a steady stream of legislation. This was also a time of intense human drama and struggle. The laws that were passed didn't simply happen or tumble out of the heads of wise and compassionate men. There is a broader context to consider.

After doing the necessary preparation—again, all the way from chronology to analyses to anecdotes—and becoming familiar with the resources available (including readings, video, and slides), block out the factual narrative. It is helpful to have students look over a simple list of key events on a reference sheet in case chronological confusion later sets in. Events that are directly related to the main themes of the unit need only briefly be mentioned since a more in-depth examination will follow.

The chronology list also provides a way to highlight some of the human interest stories that *won't* receive further attention in the unit. In the case of the Thirties, this meant having an opportunity to touch on events like the Lindbergh kidnapping case, the SS *Morro Castle* disaster, and the killing of John Dillinger—all fascinating events that contributed to the texture of the times.

Sometimes, slides would be shown to accompany this unit introduction or they might be saved for an end-of-unit review along with—please forgive the digression—causation flow charts that students would create in groups. These were essentially visual maps of the possible relationships between the facts discussed. This exercise, which can also be used for particular topics within a unit, helps students hone their critical thinking skills, bring factual information together, and create their own interpretations of the unit in graphic form. Their charts tended to be complex and often quite beautiful.

Back to unit beginnings and preliminaries. As with other units, students would first be asked what they thought the important questions were to pursue, the questions that, if answered by the end of our study, would make them feel they had learned a great deal. Since historians use salient questions to open doors to a deeper understanding of the past, this exercise helps turn students into apprentices of the trade, and it was engaging, even exciting, for them to think together as a class. Their questions would be written on the board, and then, for purposes of comparison, they would be given a list of questions that historians still debate about the period.

With the Great Depression, the unit began in earnest with students being asked to state their present views about the proper role of government as reflected in certain specific issues such as whether the government should set wages and prices, run a post office, have school systems, start enterprises that compete with private industry, bail out corporations, promote income equality, allow unions, provide healthcare, and so forth. We then discussed the responses. This exercise has several goals:

- Highlight the larger issues awaiting a student about to study the New Deal.
- Make explicit the students' assumptions and political views at the very beginning of the unit.
- Create a baseline of class views that can be compared to those at the end of the unit so students can see how, if at all, their thinking has changed.

The placement of this exercise early in the unit illustrates the importance of careful choreography in organizing a unit. If this discussion had been held later on, students would have had more difficulty separating what they had originally thought from what they later heard from others or read.

The main course to be served up, the Great Depression itself, involved considerable content for a student to learn. Some of it was lectured out. And because there was *so much* information in this "fact-y" unit, it was helpful to hand out some partially completed, "pre-fabricated," note-taking sheets to help speed things along. With this historical period, a chalk 'n' talk isn't the worst thing. By weaving in anecdotes, the teacher can still make the material more interesting than the textbook.

Still, selective text readings can also help students better assimilate the content as well as expose them to a narrative with a different perspective. (Again, the bias of the text is expressed as much by omission as by what is stated and how.) Some students will also learn better by reading than by listening.

But even the bulkiest textbook will have serious limitations, apart from its bias: an impossibly dense cosmos of facts and an impersonal narrative voice. Most likely, it will not deal meaningfully with topics like the role of the labor movement or the impact of the Depression on African Americans and women. Readings were available to deal with these more specific topics. But if time is short, lecture notes can be turned into teacher-written mini-texts, which students will invariably find livelier then the writing in their textbook. Mini-texts are also an effective way to reduce the amount of lecturing if they preserve a conversational "voice" and transmit information in a compelling way.

A unit syllabus was provided for discussions and debates, but students were always reminded that they earned their right to participate and have their views taken seriously by knowing the material. Without a reasonable command of facts, there is no story to discuss.

After researching and organizing the factual narrative and deciding the best ways to transmit or discover it (discussions, lectures, readings, etc.), attention was turned to the next curricular layer: the affective. To understand the Great Depression—why things happened, how they happened, and with what results—students have to explore how the period *felt* to those for whom this crisis was a crucible and not an academic course.

To this end, students were literally given a little taste when their teacher distributed cookies to the class based on the income distribution in 1929. How very unfair they found this! Another day was designated "Hunger Day"—with parents' permission, students who wished to skip lunch because empty stomachs provide a solid setting for discussing hungry people. Where affective education was concerned, the textbook was almost of no use— maybe worse than that.

Fortunately, the oral history of Depression-era Americans has been preserved in primary sources that include interviews, photographs, video documentaries, poems, and songs. By immersing students in this material, history itself becomes transformed. What had been a history of American presidents now becomes a history of the American people, their hopes, struggles, victories, and defeats. With the help of this material, students not only develop their capacity for empathy but also consider the possibility of themselves becoming history-makers, as many of their forebears were in the 1930s. A refrain in Walt Whitman's incomparable poem "Crossing Brooklyn Ferry" speaks to this issue:

> Lived the same life with the rest, the same old laughing, gnawing, sleeping,
> Play'd the part that still looks back on the actor or actress,
> The same old role, the role that is what we make it, as great as we like,
> Or as small as we like, or both great and small.

To study history—that immense, collective story handed down to us at such cost—is a powerful thing, and students have already been at it for several years before they arrive in high school. They know what it means to be a student, a spectator, an observer, a memorizer, a thinker, someone who "studies it." However, few see themselves as active citizens, as players, as potential participants in the making of history, as those who help to pull the levers and turn the wheels. How to convince them that history class, even at its most absorbing and entertaining, has to involve a different mind-set than watching a TV show? How to get them to consider the role they wish to play, "the role that is what we make it, as great as we like, / Or as small as we like, or both great and small." This is the challenge facing teachers.

Having students study the Bonus Expeditionary Force, the migration of the Okies, the takeover of government buildings, the bootleg mining of coal seams, the tax strikes, the squatting and looting, the Congress of Industrial Organizations drives, the sit-down strikes—all actions by desperate people—restores the Depression to a human story far broader and deeper than a list of laws and programs. As if viewing a Diego Rivera mural, we see very unordinary ordinary people trying to reshape their world across time by creating the political movements required to get all those laws passed. Past generations seem to be saying to us, "Put down that TV remote!"

The third curricular layer laid down was the analytical one, and it was interwoven with the others. (Maybe the better metaphor here is the mixing of musical tracks rather than the meandering of rivers.) It is important—and truthful—that students see history as an unresolved, contentious argument both among people living at that time and among the historians that followed. To facilitate this understanding, students need conflicting accounts and analyses. These include diverse primary sources and contrasting statistical studies as well as opposing historical interpretations. Now students had the opportunity to work through the facts and perspectives, to weigh and sift, and to reach their own conclusions in essays, classroom debates, and simulations.

In the course of this unit, students had to learn what the NIRA, CCC, and WPA were and why they were so controversial. They needed to understand the different Republican/Democratic takes on the New Deal but also to join as a class to sing "Brother, Can You Spare a Dime?" and "Dust Bowl Refugee." In an effective unit, the intellective and the affective have to embrace.

Of course, at the conclusion of this long unit, a question patiently waits for analysis and discussion: "Did the New Deal succeed?"

COURSE: TWENTIETH CENTURY AMERICAN HISTORY

Unit: The Roaring Twenties

Study the Thirties, and it will be facts to the right of you, facts to the left of you, and facts in front of you. Much as in Alfred Lord Tennyson's *The Charge of the Light Brigade*, a student must be prepared to charge in and become part of the "Noble 600." However, students, unlike heroic, obedient, and ill-fated British cavalrymen, do have the right to ask and *reason why*. Teachers should refrain from teaching material if they cannot explain its significance.

In the case of the Thirties, this is not difficult to do. So much of what students will learn prepares them to understand the political and economic landscape of their own time, including the following: the philosophical differences between Democrats/liberals, Republicans/conservatives, and radicals; the respective approaches represented by supply-side and Keynesian economics; and the relationship between the government and the citizen. The more things change, the more. . . .

The challenges posed to students by the sheer volume of facts generated by the New Deal period is somewhat balanced by the reality that most historians at least agree on the *zeitgeist* or main theme of the Thirties—it's the Great Depression all the way. In that sense, the Thirties are more straightforward, but that isn't the case with the Twenties. The contrasting nature of these two periods has implications for curriculum development.

Ask students what the Twenties were about and there's a good chance you'll hear terms like "Roaring Twenties" and "Jazz Age." But historians disagree about the nature of the Twenties *zeitgeist*, and this gives the unit an interesting twist. The issue of hypothesizing or discerning the theme therefore becomes a major focus of the unit, which involves the additional challenge of thinking conceptually.

At the beginning of the unit, when students were asked what they knew about the Twenties, they would mention things like "flappers," the "Charleston," "gangsters," "jazz," and "Prohibition." These words were duly recorded on the front board. The chronology sheets they received suggested that this high energy, happy period was actually somewhat more complex. Did the students know that the Twenties were also a time of political repression (the Palmer Raids), conservatism (Harding, Coolidge, Hoover), nativism (the Immigration Restriction Movement and the revival of the Ku Klux Klan)? In most classes, the answer was almost always "No."

After using lectures, slides, and readings to fill in the social, economic, and political background of the Twenties, the class would proceed to the issue that history and historians have carved out for us, namely, how to place the period—with its contradictory nature—under the conceptual roof of a theme. Students would then be asked, for the first but not the last time, to propose their own hypothesis.

While historians don't agree about the Twenties, there is one theory that has gained considerable support—specifically, that the period can best be characterized as a time of cultural conflict in an urbanizing, industrializing America. This is the view that informed how the unit was organized, but here students were invited to try to anticipate it or propose their own approach. At a certain point, they would be presented with one key fact and given the chance to consider how it might serve as a prism to understand the period.

That fact is this: the U.S. Census of 1920 reported that for the first time in American history, city dwellers outnumbered those living in rural areas and small towns. This fact will generate a lot of thinking in the classroom, and some students will make the conceptual leap all the way to the perspective described above—or fairly close.

Here's one possible road map for the unit:

I: Introduction

- What They Know About the Period/*Zeitgeist* Discussion
- Chronology Sheet
- Their Questions

II: Social, Economic, and Political Background

- Political: Hoover and Coolidge
- Economic: Twenties Prosperity—And Its Limits
- Social: Popular Culture, the "Lost Generation," and the Alienation of American Intellectuals

III: Searching for a Theme

IV: Arenas of Cultural Conflict

- Town vs. City: Immigrants and Sacco and Vanzetti vs. Immigration Restriction, Nativism, and Political Repression

- Science vs. City: The Scopes Trial
- Revolution in Manners and Morals vs. Moral Legislation
- Prohibition: Wets vs. Dries
- The Hoover/ Smith Election as a Metaphor of Cultural Conflict

V: Developments in the Black Community and Its Relationship to Cultural Conflict

- The Harlem Renaissance
- Marcus Garvey and Black Nationalism

This is a wonderful unit to teach. It offers rich and infinite possibilities for discussion and debate because so many issues of that period are still being discussed and debated today. For example, there's only a baby step's worth of distance between discussing the small town outrage over the revolution in morals and manners back then and discussing whether our own post-1960s era cultural revolution has gone too far. Current controversies over values closely recall the tensions of the Twenties, right down to continuing debates over sexuality, women's liberation, evolution, drinking, drugs, dress, and dance. Issues concerning immigrants and nativism fairly leap out of the pages of this decade and onto our students' desks.

In some respects, liberals and conservatives, and the more urbanized Blue States and small-town Red States, are still engaged in the same "culture wars" that began in the Twenties. Students will not need much encouragement to dive into these debates that are so historical *and* contemporary at the same time. Indeed, the wall dividing past and present in this unit seems almost ready to tumble down. Simple handouts listing topics like grinding, song lyrics, sex ed in schools, creationism, dress codes, drug/drinking policies, and the various proposed solutions, are more than sufficient for heated and sustained discussions.

Some of the anxieties of Americans in the Twenties seem laughable to us now. But others appear startlingly close to home and will inevitably raise questions about just how far we have travelled in the past century. The strong feelings that students have about the same or analogous issues demonstrate how historical controversies can persist and remain for later generations to wrestle with and resolve.

Throw in a Charleston contest, and you have a unit.

COURSE: POSTWAR AMERICA—THE FIFTIES AND SIXTIES

Unit: "The Great Postponement" (or How the Quiet Fifties Birthed the Turbulent Sixties)

The Postwar course grew out of a problem quite well known to history teachers. It's called running out of time. The end of year comes rearing up out of nowhere, and you always seem to be stuck once again in that catastrophic place known as World War II. The Postwar course was devoted to the Fifties and Sixties, periods which usually got scant coverage during my career. One of the first units, "The Great Postponement" (thank you, historian Geoffrey Hodgson, for that phrase and concept) focuses on the subterranean and suppressed discontents of the Fab Fifties that would later explode into the Sixties.

Again, the unit begins with a description of the factual landscape. The general techniques described above apply here as well, so only a few special aspects will be highlighted. This unit focused on three topics: "Dissenting Intellectuals," "The Rise of the Teenager," and "The Beats." (The connection of all three with African Americans and the civil rights movement was discussed, but this momentous topic was largely spun off into its own unit.)

During the fearful and conformist Fifties, seeds of dissent were planted by a handful of intellectuals and writers who lent a critical eye to our emerging postwar society. Books like *The Organization Man*; *The Power Elite*; *The Lonely Crowd*; and, later, *The Feminine Mystique*; *The Other America*; *and Silent Spring* raised critical questions about American life at a time when such questioning was not invited or welcomed. During the following decade, these critiques would become more widely shared.

Dealing with this subtopic was an object lesson about the value of minimalism in curriculum creation, something this teacher hadn't always taken to heart. (Yes, too much curriculum, even the best, can crowd out student discussion.) Students received a handout with brief summaries of the books, and on the basis of that one sheet, the class had very rich discussions about whether the issues raised by the authors were still relevant today and also whether books still played a significant role in shaping how the students viewed their society and world.

Our study of teens was more extensive—and even more fun. Here modified lecture and brief readings in class—the longer ones being reserved for homework—provided historical context and multiple interpretations. Personal anecdotes were particularly useful in conveying the texture and tone of the period. Throughout our study of this new demographic/cultural subgroup, there were many opportunities to discuss the universals of the teen experience but also to contrast the lives and consciousness of teens then and now.

We sang some Golden Oldies together. The music was used not only to help impart the "feel" of the period as in other units but as primary documents that helped to reveal the alienation, anxiety, restlessness, and racism of the dominant culture. Watching key scenes from *Rebel without a Cause* and *Blackboard Jungle* added a dimension that pried students' eyes wide open. (And if that didn't wake them up, the surprise classroom "switchblade" comb-knife fight that began when the lights were turned on certainly did.)

What most distinguished this topic from other history units was the central role given to two novels, J. D. Salinger's *Catcher in the Rye* ("Teens") and Jack Kerouac's *On the Road* ("the Beats"), as well as a selection of Beat poetry that all students were required to read. It's fairly routine for a history teacher to assign a book report for homework, but to use literature as central texts for history curricula is less common.

Using novels as the spine for this unit helped frame the historical material as problems. What our English Department colleagues always knew came as something of a revelation: literature makes it easier to get across concepts like interpretation, perspective, and point of view. (Here too, time is the enemy of "best practices," which is why fiction isn't used more widely in history classes. In the Great Depression unit, students were assigned one pivotal chapter in Steinbeck's *The Grapes of Wrath*, and that also worked well.)

Novels give students a way to enter into history and to ponder what they might have said or done in a particular situation. The way fiction expresses the "feel" and sensibility of a time period encourages students to become more nuanced in their thinking. After all, the ambivalences and contradictions that characters present cannot be ignored. For students to understand these books, they have to first figure out what's going on in the narrative and then look below the surface. Of course, this is the same skill that is required in historical study.

Our discussions tried to unlock the meaning of the books and poems. Was *The Catcher in the Rye* an ahistorical, psychological study of a lonely postwar teen or a critique of his times? Was Holden a sympathetic character? Was *On the Road* a celebration of all things hedonistic and a flight from responsibility? Or was it the story of one man's search for meaning? What did Kerouac himself make of his early adventures? Beyond the light these discussions shed on the Fifties and on the Beats, the use of literature also opened up additional creative opportunities. Some students wrote imaginative, "newly discovered" chapters from *On the Road*. Others wrote the story of their youth in the style of Allen Ginsberg's "Howl" or their versions of his famous poem "America" and shared them with classmates, with jazz playing quietly in our darkened room. One student wrote a wonderful song based on a few lines from *On the Road* and sang it to guitar and drum accompaniment. Kerouac would have loved it.

In the course of this unit, students were asked to consider historical interpretations, literature, music, and other primary sources. They were asked to think, to imagine, and to lift their voices in discussion and song.

The story of the underlying fissures that developed in the Fifties is intriguing to be sure. Through the lens of this unit, students could begin to understand where the Sixties came from, how that turbulent time emerged from the conformist "Silent Generation" (or the supposedly carefree Fab Fifties). This was a unit that provided easy access for students to enter into history. On exiting, they often felt they had also gained more clarity on their own values, aspirations, and search for meaning.

Every teacher has a different process for developing and organizing curriculum. But even diverse approaches have this much in common: lesson- and unit-planning must be a continuous process, informed by study and honest self-criticism. The perfect lesson has yet to be created, and there is always room for improvement.

Educators "play" in front of tough and demanding audiences so there is considerable incentive to improve pedagogy and curriculum. Teachers can't control which students will take their courses, and each class will have its own challenging dynamics. Thoughtfully shaped, interesting, and exciting lessons and units are among the few variables over which teachers can exercise some control.

Chapter Fifteen

Not Just Civics Class, But a Civic Life

Democracy Makes Its Demands

At the heart of Dewey's educational philosophy was the importance of preparing students for democratic citizenship. He stressed that consciously guided education aimed at developing the "mental equipment" and moral character of students was essential to the development of civic character . . . The best way to do this, he said, was to introduce students at the outset to "a mode of associated living" characteristic of democracy. A school should be a community of full participation and "conjoint communicated experience" in which social sympathy and deliberative moral reason would develop.

—Scott London, *Organic Democracy: The Political Philosophy of John Dewey*

Let's go back to the beginning.

Why do we want high school students to learn history in the first place? It's not the memorization, is it? Surely most won't remember much of the material for very long unless they take additional courses in college (where, *sigh*, few will choose to become history majors). Still, there are facts, themes, topics, and chronology that must be taught unless we are prepared to accept historical illiteracy as well as the lack of self-knowledge and the powerlessness that necessarily follow.

Then there are the many habits of mind and academic skills that historical study helps to develop: assimilating content, analyzing and evaluating arguments, constructing an interpretation, being able to think logically and to reject the specious, writing clearly, and so on. Perhaps there's also some

159

empathy to be gained along the way. And maybe, just maybe we actually will learn *something* to prevent us from making the "same mistakes" that have turned so many centuries crimson. One can hope.

Where civics is concerned, students need to be familiar with the founding documents of the American experiment, our constitutional system, and democratic values. How can we expect students to tend and protect our democracy if they don't understand at least the basics? But they also need their studies to help them understand how our political system *actually* works (or doesn't), quite apart from the theory. That splatter of reality rarely appears in those neat and tidy charts listing the constitutional checks and balances or in curricula too often mired in the arcane details of constitutional minutiae. *Letters of marque and reprisal anyone?*

The other aspect of civics that too frequently gets ignored is the opportunity—and need—for students to participate meaningfully in the life of their school and country. This is a significant omission because it is participation that teaches democratic habits and behavior. Without this dimension of learning, civics can easily become "just talk," and kids know the difference. Being involved in issues that matter to them helps them to grow and learn to take responsibility. "Just talk"—whether in civics class or in student governments that are mainly stagecraft—keeps them, well, kids.

Many schools today face a civics infrastructure challenge. They need to create meaningful connections within the school community and also broad avenues to the outside world. At Lincoln-Sudbury, we tried to accomplish this in a number of different ways.

SERVICE AND THE MARTIN LUTHER KING ACTION PROGRAM

Service programs can offer just such an avenue and we had—and still have—an excellent one at Lincoln-Sudbury called the Martin Luther King Action Project (MLKAP). Through it, student volunteers travel throughout the Boston area to help in soup kitchens, shelters, and food banks. MLKAP also sponsors an annual memorial/fundraising AIDS march, Thanksgiving dinners for the elderly, an alternative April vacation Habitat for Humanity program in Philadelphia, and a community service week for seniors. Through MLKAP, students can fulfill Lincoln-Sudbury's modest service requirement and, hopefully, through their experiences, deepen their compassion and active concern for others. MLKAP has long helped isolated suburban youth become sensitized to a very different world that is not very geographically distant from their own.

RESPONDING TO DEVELOPMENTS IN THE WORLD

When oppression persists or disaster strikes, students don't need to be prodded to help. They want to be involved. What schools need to provide is time and space. From 1970 to 1990, there was an active student group at Lincoln-Sudbury called "Students Against Apartheid." For a decade, they helped educate the school community about South Africa. Particularly noteworthy was the year kids built a Soweto-type shantytown outside the school. Another year they held a demonstration at the old town center—not a typical scene in an affluent suburb.

When the great South Asian tsunami of 2004 struck and, a year later, Hurricane Katrina, students mobilized to raise relief funds. The administration permitted them to transform the largest public space in the school. In the case of the tsunami, walls were papered with 150,000 copies of photos from the school yearbook to give the community a sense of what the enormous toll meant in human terms. A similar effort was made with Katrina, and for some years after students traveled to New Orleans on vacation breaks to help with the rebuilding effort.

EXTRACURRICULAR CLUBS

Over the years, the Lincoln-Sudbury culture has been enriched by a host of clubs focused on specific concerns: interracial and interfaith dialogue (Breaking Barriers and Colors); sexual orientation and equality (Gay/Straight Alliance); and international crises (Stop Genocide in Darfur, and Free Tibet); and local support (Sudbury Angels). The high school also had a Young Democratic Club and a student ACLU as well as Amnesty International. Each of these groups tried to disseminate information and organize around their issues through petitions, presentations, and fundraising.

With all these activities, teachers helped provide guidance and structure, but students made the decisions. That's a fine line, but it needs to be respected whenever possible.

THE STUDENT NEWSPAPER

There can be no civic life or democratic society without newspapers and a free press. In 1988, in the *Hazelwood School District vs. Kuhlmeier* decision, the U.S. Supreme Court restricted the free speech rights of high school journalists. Fortunately, this wasn't the last word for all high school students. In four states, including Massachusetts, the legislature restored these rights to student journalists. Lincoln-Sudbury's school newspaper was never censored, and in fact, no administrators even saw the latest issue until it was delivered to their mailbox.

Alas, the freedom that our student journalists took for granted at Lincoln-Sudbury is unknown at many American high schools. This is unfortunate. Most school newspaper advisers will affirm that students can exercise the rights of a free press in a responsible manner. Again, the best way we can teach the value of democratic rights is by permitting, even encouraging, students to actually use them.

At Lincoln-Sudbury, a test case of this freedom came when the unthinkable occurred. In 2007, a student was murdered at the school. The school community was traumatized. The staff of the school paper, the *Forum*, immediately started working on a special issue. When faculty heard about this effort, several asked the principal to intervene and forbid it. They feared that a special issue would only intensify the emotional climate of the school. The student editors, however, insisted on their right to be journalists and report the news.

The principal supported them, and when students and staff returned to school after the weekend, each received a copy of the Lincoln-Sudbury student newspaper. Everyone on the faculty agreed the special issue showed sensitivity, thoroughness, and accuracy. These student journalists had risen to this tragic occasion.

SPECIAL SCHOOL PROJECTS AND TRIPS

The field trips to Washington, DC, and to the Deep South (see chapter 4) were also expressions of civic concern. Today Lincoln-Sudbury is experimenting with a Global Scholars program. Trips have been organized to the Dominican Republic, Tanzania, Japan, and Cambodia, most of them combining service with cultural exchange.

In Cambodia, students and alumni worked together to build a new schoolhouse for children in a poor village. Lincoln-Sudbury Memorial School, which opened in 2010, helps the youth of Cambodia in the name of the students and alumni of Lincoln-Sudbury who died before their time. This living memorial—which began as one student's inspired idea—is a powerful expression of global citizenship and continues to be financially supported by student and alumni fundraising.

ANNIVERSARIES ... AGAIN

The importance of a school community observing significant anniversaries bears repeating because civics education makes as strong a claim on these events as history classes. The fiftieth anniversary of the end of World War II? Time for students to plant a tree or to invite veterans in. Abraham Lincoln's birthday? Classes in any and all subjects should begin by reading some of his eloquent words. Pearl Harbor Day? Let's hear FDR's announcement on the PA system. Anniversary of 9/11? At the very least, students should be invited to participate in a moment of silence. Civics, no less than history, is about remembering.

PARTICIPATING IN THE LIFE OF A DEMOCRACY

Teachers should work to ensure that students are allowed—even encouraged—to take positions on current controversies, if they feel so moved, whether by circulating petitions or lobbying on a range of issues such as the Iraq War, gay marriage, genocide in Darfur, and gun violence. Classroom simulations are no substitute for the real thing. However, caution is required. Teachers have a significant role to play in asking questions, encouraging reflection, and providing guidance and structure. They shouldn't stifle student initiatives, if lawful and non-disruptive, but they should help students think through tactics and goals.

In 2004, there were strong feelings—pro and con—among students at Lincoln-Sudbury concerning gay marriage. A historic change was being proposed in Massachusetts. How should a school respond to such a polarizing issue? The school organized buses so students could travel to the state house to lobby legislators in support or in opposition to the proposed reform. Student representatives of both positions traveled together to voice their opinions. In this way, Democracy Day provided an important civics experience for all those who participated.

THE CONTINUING CHALLENGE OF CIVICS

Civic life continues to have a presence at Lincoln-Sudbury, as it does at many other schools, but it could be stronger. Budget cuts imperil it. The shadows cast by a culture obsessed with college admission and material wealth are powerful. Civic activities are still seen as "extras" without the status or support received by the athletic program. Ironically, "civility"—a favorite conflict-avoidance buzzword—enjoys wide currency. Sometimes school committees forget that it is the vibrancy of civic life that creates the need for civility. Civility presupposes civics.

Under the best of circumstances, creating a democratic, civic consciousness in public education is not easy. Adults want young people to do what they say, not what they do, and too often Americans define themselves more as consumers than citizens. A large number of us can't be bothered to vote. Even in Sudbury, Massachusetts, one of the original Puritan towns that introduced town meeting governance to the world, fewer and fewer people bother to attend the annual event. Red Sox Nation doesn't appear to share this problem. Schools have a wide chasm to bridge.

However, teachers have to build that bridge. They must persist. And the most important first step is rededicating ourselves to the democratic values we hope to impart to our students. A vibrant, self-renewing democracy requires active young citizens. The epic story related in U.S. history courses about our long, continuing struggle to create "a more perfect union" and to achieve "liberty and justice for all" must become more than just a tale told in a fourth-block class.

Encouraging students to help write the next chapter of our national story should be part of a school's core educational mission, and teachers have to take the lead. Maybe they will get some extra-duty pay, but more certainly they will have the opportunity to work with and come to know their students in a fuller way and to "cast their influence," as Thoreau would put it, more widely.

"Must," "should," and "have to" are harsh words that have the ring of commands. But how else will students learn democratic values? They need the chance to do meaningful work and take brave stands on behalf of peers, neighbors, fellow Americans, and all of suffering humanity.

So no make-believe allowed. As one alumnus recently wrote to his former teachers: "Please keep it real." There are few pedagogical ideas more deserving to be honored.

Epilogue

Actually, There Is No Ending

One child, one teacher, one book, one pen can change the world.
—Malala Yousafzai, *I Am Malala*

My teaching career concluded in 2008 when my emeritus teaching stint ended. Many times since people have asked, "Do you miss the classroom?" and each time the honest response is "Yes—though not so much the grading!" Those thirty-five years spent as a classroom teacher never felt like anything less than a great privilege and high responsibility.

So why leave? Perhaps for the same reason that Thoreau gave for leaving Walden Pond after his idyllic two years, two months, and two days there. After spending nearly three hundred pages describing his Walden Pond–side paradise in his classic of the same name, he abruptly announced his departure. In the last chapter of the book, "Conclusion," Thoreau explained why he decided to go. "I left the woods," he wrote, "for as good a reason as I went there. Perhaps it seemed to me that I had several more lives to live, and could not spare any more time for that one."

It was no easier to leave Lincoln-Sudbury Regional High School than it was for Thoreau to leave his beloved Walden Woods. The school had an informal and warm culture: no bells, no dress codes, no honor roll, free periods when students could hang out in hallways or meet with teachers. Academically, the emphasis was placed on encouraging a love of learning.

The school motto captured the prevailing ethos: Think for Yourself, but Think of Others. A similar culture of education can be found in a few other suburban high schools around Massachusetts, as well as a remarkable Boston public school called the Boston Arts Academy. Suburbs do not—and need not—have a monopoly on progressive educational ideas or engaging school cultures.

In the course of its sixty-five-year history, Lincoln-Sudbury made three great discoveries about how best to invest teachers and students in teaching and learning.

First, by giving students a measure of free time, they had the chance to forge strong relationships with teachers outside the classroom and to feel respected as the young adults they are.

Second, by allowing students to choose electives—beyond the required courses—they were given the opportunity to cultivate interests and follow their passions.

Third, by according the faculty considerable academic freedom, the possibility of occasionally creating new courses, and having input into hiring and policy decisions, the school invested teachers in their work and gave them a sense of ownership. The course you taught was *your* course. Lincoln-Sudbury teachers and students spoke of the school as "ours." Teachers were highly motivated because they were treated as professionals, as members of the community, and not merely as employees.

But it was time to leave. For almost four decades, my passion found a home in the history classroom. Was there really another life out there for me to live? One could hope!

Working with young people can be habit forming though, so it shouldn't have been too surprising that the search for those other lives led back into schools, first as a practicum supervisor for student-teachers from Tufts University and the University of Massachusetts, Boston, then as a Wheelock College mentor for Boston teachers, and last as a volunteer tutor in a Boston public school. For five years, I also worked as a court-appointed special advocate (CASA) investigating child-abuse cases for the state, a role that brought me into schools as well. These responsibilities, as significant as they were, could not compare to the engrossing daily challenge of classroom teaching.

These last words are meant especially for my fellow teachers. They deserve our collective thanks for taking on the difficult and critical work of educating new generations of young people. That's a sentiment most parents would agree with, and it is stated with the confidence and sincerity of a teacher who is also a parent.

The other day an old National Public Radio interview with Jerry Seinfeld was rebroadcast. The interviewer asked why, after all his success, he still does stand-up comedy, with all the risks of failure pertaining thereto. Seinfeld responded simply, "I don't want to cheat." He went on to explain that he didn't want to take shortcuts or ride on his past fame.

The same goes for teachers. "Cheating" or shortcuts are definitely not allowed. You will possibly not get as much sleep as you might wish, but there's only one way to do this job, and that is to keep it real, to go the distance, and to do it fully. To do the best you can.

Like anything else, teaching has its mundane moments, its rainy weeks, and its thankless bureaucratic requirements, but the creative possibilities are endless. So despite some discouraging "reforms" that disempower teachers, those contemplating a career in the classroom are still to be envied. Teachers and educators-to-be, students will be grateful for your inspired efforts! I still think of my old teachers with gratitude.

And those students . . . those incredible young people! Being entrusted to teach them about the past is such an honor and responsibility. Why work a job, when a calling is possible?

The vista created in a classroom can be as limitless, breathtaking, and as mind-expanding as history itself. In the end, Whitman's "dark unfathom'd retrospect" can be illuminated only by teachers who refuse to surrender their imagination to soulless curriculum frameworks and relentless testing. It's harder to be creative now and takes more wit than now-retired teachers ever had to muster. But consider the way water flows and finds a channel. History expects no less of you.

One of the many current buzzwords in educational circles is "21st-century skills." But teachers know that the challenge of providing a meaningful education remains more or less the same. It will always involve teaching skills, encouraging thoughtful habits of mind, imparting content, broadening a sense of humanity, and deepening the natural curiosity that all children have. As always, these goals will require teachers with knowledge and commitment.

And maybe, also, courage.

Coda

To Be a Teacher

To be a teacher,
to crawl into your classroom
on a boggy Monday,
to try to light a fire with
wet matches,
to strike and strike again,
to see a flicker of light
in the eye of a student,
to blow softly on the
embers,
to see them blown out
with the wrong words,
then roar to life with
a question well put.

To be a teacher,
to strike and strike
again.

April 23, 2005

About the Author

Bill Schechter was born in 1946, grew up in the Bronx, and attended P.S. 95, J.H.S. 143, and DeWitt Clinton High School. He graduated from Cornell University and did graduate work in history at the University of California, Berkeley, and Harvard University. He received a master's in history and teaching from Goddard College.

After completing his student-teaching at Brighton High School in 1973, Bill was hired by the Lincoln-Sudbury Regional High School History Department and remained at the school for thirty-five years. In the course of his career, he received a number of honors, including finalist designation for the Massachusetts Department of Education's Louisa Crocker Award (1990); a Faculty Recognition Award from the Class of 1992; the Outstanding Educator Award from Cornell University (2002); and a METCO Recognition Award (2006).

Five years after his retirement, Bill's name was placed on Lincoln-Sudbury's Wall of Recognition. He considers it his greatest honor to have served as a classroom teacher. In retirement, he was privileged to work as a practicum supervisor for Tufts University and for the University of Massachusetts, Boston, helping to launch new teachers into the classroom.

His early interest in history was encouraged by his parents, his immigrant grandparents, and his New York City public school teachers. He is still grateful that the P.S. 95 library allowed him to borrow a biography of Yankee immortal Lou Gehrig.

Throughout his study of history, a belief—or is it a hope—has endured that we must study history, not only because, as Abraham Lincoln observed, we cannot escape it, but because possibly, just possibly, we can find meaning in history, learn something from it, and use those lessons to make the world better for generations to come.

Bill is married, has two grown sons, and lives in Brookline, Massachusetts.